Johnson Brothers
Classic English Dinnerware

by
Bob Page
Dale Frederiksen

Page/Frederiksen Publications
Greensboro, North Carolina
With Price Guide

ACKNOWLEDGMENTS

Book projects at Replacements, Ltd. require the efforts of many people, both Replacements' staff and those from outside the company who share information with us. We wish to sincerely thank each of you, however large or small your part may have been, and whether or not your name appears in the list below. Some people who merit a special thank you include:

Dean Six, Researcher
Todd Hall, Photographer
Cindy Allred, Imaging Department Manager
Sherry Blankenship, Graphic Artist
Rachael Potts, Graphic Artist
Rob Fisher, Project Specialist
Roberta Newman, Sara Barringer,
Cora Miller, Pat West, Chris Kirkman and
the Attributing and Research staffs
Mary Finegan

FRONT COVER
Platter: **Heritage Hall–Brown/Multicolor**
Pitcher: **The Florentine–Green**
Dinner Plate: **Old Britain Castles–Pink**
Cup & Saucer Set: **His Majesty**
Covered Vegetable Bowl: **Claremont** (Flow Blue)
Gravy Ladle: **Neapolitan** (Flow Blue, Gold Accents)

BACK COVER
Back Row, left to right: Platter, **Richmond**; Dinner Plate, **Kenworth**; Platter, **Florida**.
Middle Row, left to right: Round Covered Vegetable Bowl, **Mongolia**; Tureen, **Royston**; Sugar Bowl with Lid, **Astoria**; Round Covered Butter Dish, **The Blue Danube**.
Front Row, left to right: Bone Dish, **Oxford**; Gravy Boat with Underplate, **The Trieste**; Cereal Bowl, **Argyle**; Cup & Saucer Set, **Turin**, Butter Pat, **The Jewel**.

PUBLISHED BY:
Page/Frederiksen Publications
Greensboro, North Carolina

Copyright © 2003 by Page/Frederiksen Publications
ALL RIGHTS RESERVED
No part of this book may be reproduced without the expressed
written permission of the authors and publishers.

Additional copies of this book may be ordered from:

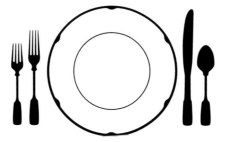

REPLACEMENTS, LTD.
China, Crystal & Silver • Old & New

1089 Knox Road • PO Box 26029 • Greensboro, North Carolina 27420
1-800-737-5223 (1-800-REPACE)
www.replacements.com®

Table of Contents

Acknowledgments 2
How to Find Your Pattern 3
Johnson Brothers History 4-5
Plate Shape Illustrations
    Scalloped Rim Shapes 6-10
    Smooth Rim Shapes 10-11
    Coupe Shapes 11
Pattern Layouts 12
Patterns
    Scalloped Rim Shapes 13-116
    Smooth Rim Shapes 117-169
    Coupe Shapes 170-190
Multi-Motif Patterns 191-194
Backstamp Samples 195
Index 196-202
About The Authors 203
Replacements, Ltd. History 204-205
Other Publications and Resources 206-208

How To Find Your Pattern

This book is organized to enable you to find patterns using the SHAPE of your dinner plate. We have created a visual index that uses a simple line drawing of the dinner plate shapes made by Johnson Brothers. These will guide you to the likely section where your pattern can be found. Sample shapes are organized in three groups: Scalloped shapes, Smooth Rim shapes, and Coupe shapes. Some of the "shapes" have names taken from manufacturer information or other literature (i.e., Heritage or Richmond), while other unidentified shapes have been given numbers assigned by Replacements. Finding the shape of your pattern in the visual index will help narrow down your search and direct you to the page(s) in the book where these patterns are located.

We were not able to attribute a shape for all patterns. For those with an unknown shape, we have presented them in their own layouts within their broader categories (Scalloped, Smooth Rim, Coupe), and have organized them according to their characteristics. When a shape or grouping had a large number of patterns, we tried to divide that selection into smaller searchable layouts by grouping patterns with similar traits. For instance, a general layout of coupe shaped patterns is further divided into two layouts by whether or not there is a floral design on the pattern.

Pattern information in this guide is given under each individual pattern image and may include the pattern name, pattern number, or some type of description. Many patterns shown here have not been identified from the manufacturer or from literature. For those we have not been able to identify we have assigned "JB" numbers (i.e., JB135 or JB233). These numbers were assigned by Replacements in sequence as the patterns were found and are used to categorize and catalog patterns with unknown names.

The History of Johnson Brothers China

In 1883 two brothers, Alfred and Frederick Johnson, purchased a defunct pottery known as the Charles Street Works in Hanley, England. Hanley is in the midst of the well recognized English pottery district known as Staffordshire.

The brothers already had ties to the pottery business. The young Johnson brothers' father had married the daughter of a master potter, James Meakin, and the boys learned their trade working in and around the family business. The new firm added brother Robert in 1888. The last remaining brother, Henry, became a partner in 1893. The partnership of the four brothers lasted a short time; Alfred left to establish his own pottery around 1896.

Johnson Brothers' success seems to have been quickly established as they underwent considerable expansion in a short period of time. In 1889 they completed work on a new plant called the Hanley Pottery. Shortly thereafter, the Alexander Pottery was constructed and in 1891 the Imperial Works Pottery was added. A final expansion came in 1896 with the Trent Sanitary Works which was dedicated to manufacturing products other than tableware. These factories were all in close proximity to one another. By the end of the 1890s Johnson Brothers may have been the largest earthenware manufacturer in the world. In this early period both their white ware, popular in America, and Flow Blue were major products.

Expansion and sales were slowed by World War I, but production increased again in the 1930s. The introduction of patterns made of a solid color clay in a line called "Dawn" and off white colored patterns called "Pareek ware" helped increase sales. Patterns made with both these clays remained popular for decades.

Top Right: *Tokio pattern; an example of a flow blue pattern.*

Bottom Left: *Greydawn–Blue pattern; an example of a solid colored pattern in the "Dawn" line.*

Next Page Top Right: *Adam pattern; an example of a popular "pareek ware" pattern.*

Next Page Bottom: *pages from a Marshall Fields & Company, promotional brochure, c. 1940s.*

In 1970, Johnson Brothers china was issued a royal warrant which allows the company to supply ware to England's Queen Elizabeth. In a nation of exceptional potteries, a royal warrant is a coveted honor and indicates great respect and regard for a company's product.

Johnson Brothers china became a part of the Wedgwood Group in 1968 joining Adams, Coalport, Mason, Meakin, Midwinter, and others to work cooperatively. A member of the Johnson family sits on the board of the Wedgwood Company. Since 1986, Johnson Brothers has been a part of the Waterford-Wedgwood group of companies. In the summer of 2003 the Waterford-Wedgwood group announced they would close the Eagle Pottery in Hanley and the Alexander Pottery at Tunstall by year's end. These traditional and historic sources for the production of Johnson Brothers ware are being closed in a movement toward "multi-sourcing" the products to production firms abroad. Johnson Brothers ware is expected to be made in China and other possible markets around the globe by the beginning of 2004.

For further or more detailed reading about Johnson Brothers, we suggest two sources upon which much of the above is dependent and we hereby acknowledge their research:

VanBuskirk, William H., *Later Victorian Flow Blue and Other Ceramic Wares: A Selected History of Potteries and Shapes*. Atglen PA, Schiffer Publishing, 2002.

Finegan, Mary J., *Johnson Brothers Dinnerware: Pattern Directory & Price Guide*. Privately published. Boone NC, 2003.

Johnson Brothers Plate Illustrations

Scalloped Rim Shapes

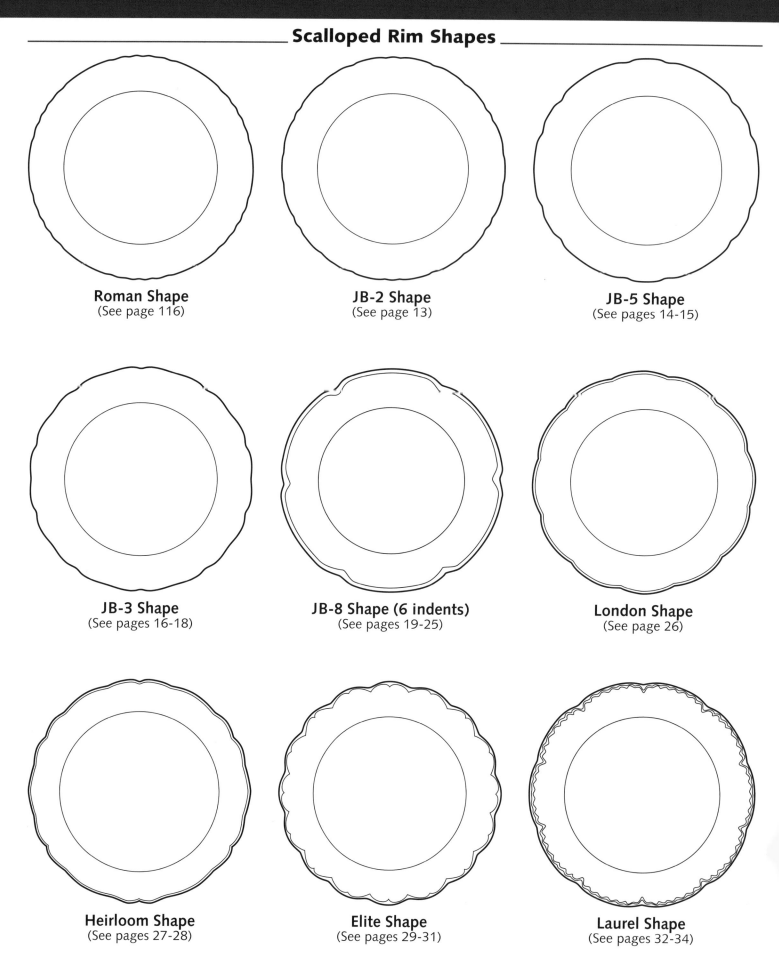

Roman Shape (See page 116)

JB-2 Shape (See page 13)

JB-5 Shape (See pages 14-15)

JB-3 Shape (See pages 16-18)

JB-8 Shape (6 indents) (See pages 19-25)

London Shape (See page 26)

Heirloom Shape (See pages 27-28)

Elite Shape (See pages 29-31)

Laurel Shape (See pages 32-34)

Johnson Brothers Plate Illustrations

Scalloped Rim Shapes

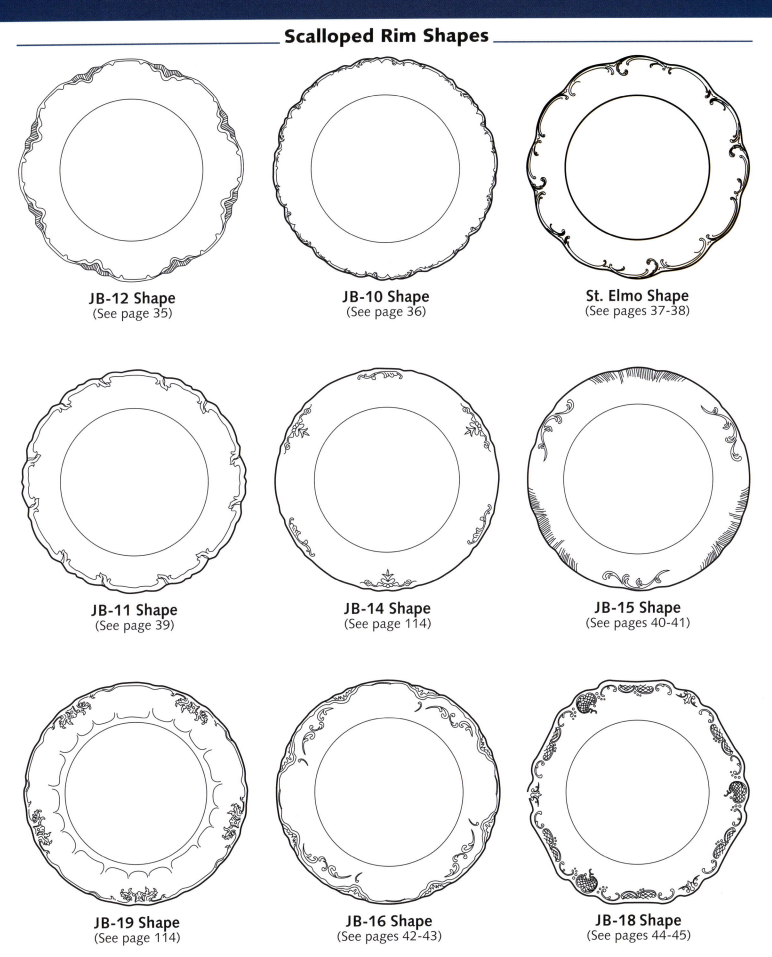

7

Johnson Brothers Plate Illustrations

Scalloped Rim Shapes

JB-20 Shape
(See page 46)

JB-17 Shape
(See page 114)

Erminie Shape
(See pages 47-48)

Silver Shape
(See pages 49-51)

JB-21 Shape
(See pages 52-54)

Old English Shape
(See pages 55-65)

Old English (Scalloped) Shape
(See page 66)

JB-6 Shape
(See pages 67-68)

Old Staffordshire Shape
(See pages 69-72)

Johnson Brothers Plate Illustrations

Scalloped Rim Shapes

Old Staffordshire 1 Shape
(See pages 73-74)

Old Staffordshire 2 Shape
(See page 75)

Old Staffordshire 3 Shape
(See pages 76-77)

Richmond Shape
(See page 78)

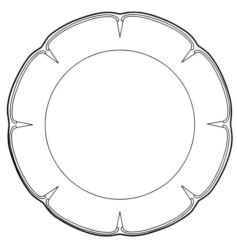

Georgian Shape
(See pages 79-81)

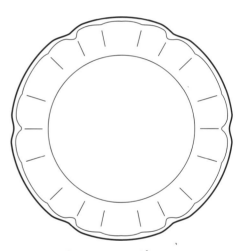

Sovereign Shape
(See pages 82-90)

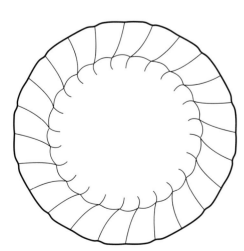

Old Chelsea Shape
(See pages 91-96)

Regency Shape
(See pages 97-106)

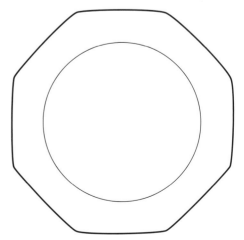

JB-28 Shape
(See pages 107-108)

Johnson Brothers Plate Illustrations

Scalloped Rim Shapes

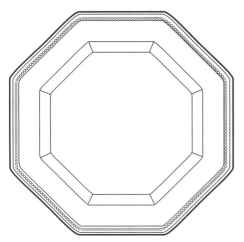

Heritage Shape
(See pages 109-111)

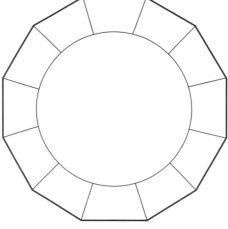

JB-27 Shape
(See pages 112-113)

Miscellaneous Scalloped Rim Shaped Patterns (Shape Unknown)
(See pages 114-116)

Smooth Rim Shapes

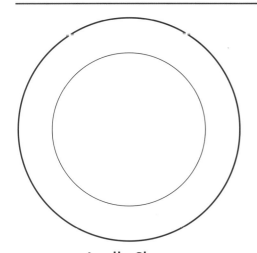

Apollo Shape
(See page 157)

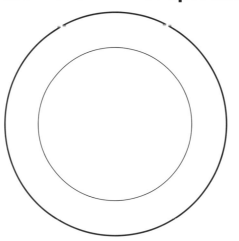

Classic Shape
(See page 157)

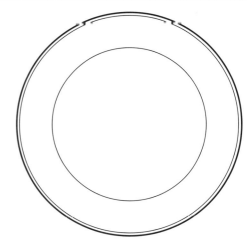

Colonial Shape
(See page 157)

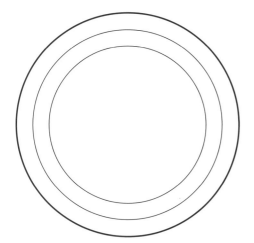

Roulette Shape
(See page 157)

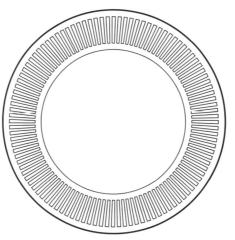

Athena (or Viking) Shape
(See pages 117-118)

JB-26 Shape
(See pages 119-120)

Johnson Brothers Plate Illustrations

Smooth Rim Shapes

Miscellaneous Smooth Rim Shaped Patterns (Shape Unknown)
(See pages 121-169)

Coupe Shapes

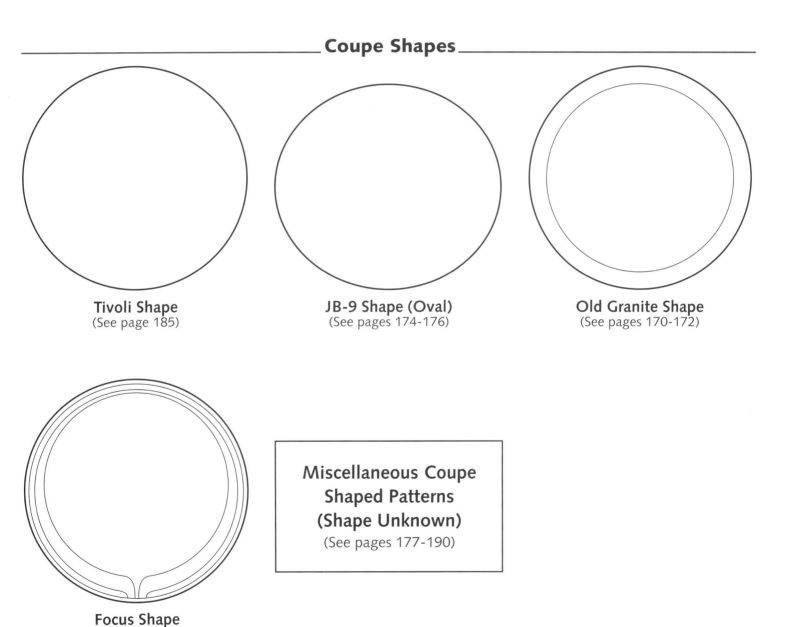

Tivoli Shape
(See page 185)

JB-9 Shape (Oval)
(See pages 174-176)

Old Granite Shape
(See pages 170-172)

Focus Shape
(See page 173)

Miscellaneous Coupe Shaped Patterns (Shape Unknown)
(See pages 177-190)

Pattern Layouts

Scalloped Rim Shapes

JB-2 Shape	13
JB-5 Shape	14-15
JB-3 Shape	16-18
JB-8 Shape	19-25
London Shape	26
Heirloom Shape	27-28
Elite Shape	29-31
Laurel Shape	32-34
JB-12 Shape	35
JB-10 Shape	36
St. Elmo Shape	37-38
JB-11 Shape	39
JB-15 Shape	40-41
JB-16 Shape	42-43
JB-18 Shape	44-45
JB-20 Shape	46
Erminie Shape	47-48
Silver Shape	49-51
JB-21 Shape	52-54
Old English Shape	55-65
Old English Scalloped Shape	66
JB-6 Shape	67-68
Old Staffordshire Shape	69-72
Old Staffordshire 1 Shape	73-74
Old Staffordshire 2 Shape	75
Old Staffordshire 3 Shape	76-77
Richmond Shape	78
Georgian Shape	79-81
Sovereign Shape	82-90
Old Chelsea Shape	91-96
Regency Shape	97-106
JB-28 Shape	107-108
Heritage Shape	109-111
JB-27 Shape	112-113
Miscellaneous (Shape Unknown)	114-116

Smooth Rim Shapes

Athena (Viking) Shape	117-118
JB26 Shape	119-120
Miscellaneous (Shape Unknown)	
Floral, Middle Design, Gold Trim	121-127
Floral, No Middle Design, Gold Trim	128-142
Non-Floral, Gold Trim	143-148
Platinum or Other Trim	149-156
No Trim	157-169

Coupe Shapes

Old Granite Shape	170-172
Focus Shape	173
JB-9 Shape (Oval)	174-176
Miscellaneous (Shape Unknown)	
Floral	177-184
Non-Floral	185-190

Multi-Motif Patterns ... 191-194

(Scalloped) JB-2 Shape

Wild Turkeys–Flying
No Trim

Wild Turkeys–Brown
Native American
No Trim

Woodland Wild Turkeys–Brown/Multicolor
No Trim

Woodland Wild Turkeys–Green
No Trim

Winter Holiday
No Trim

Harvest
No Trim

JB-5 Shape (Scalloped)

Leighton–Blue
Soup Bowl Shown
No Trim

Leighton–Gray
Soup Bowl Shown
No Trim

Leighton–Brown
Luncheon Plate Shown
No Trim

Hop
No Trim

Convolvulus
Luncheon Plate Shown
No Trim

Sylvan–Blue
Salad Plate Shown
No Trim

Sylvan–Brown
No Trim

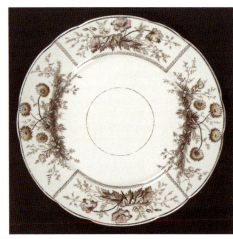
Sylvan–Brown/Multicolor
Luncheon Plate Shown
Gold Trim

Peach–Brown
No Trim

(Scalloped) JB-5 Shape

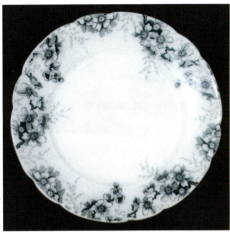
Peach–Flow Blue
No Trim

Khyber
Soup Bowl Shown
No Trim

Paris–Blue/Green
Luncheon Plate Shown
No Trim

Paris–Brown
No Trim

Rosedale
No Trim

JB448
No Trim

JB672
Luncheon Plate Shown
No Trim

JB485
Bone Dish Shown
No Trim

Columbia
Luncheon Plate Shown
No Trim

JB-3 Shape (Scalloped)

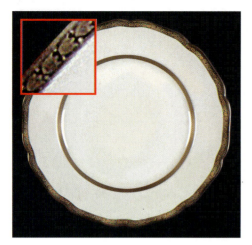
JB267
Gold Trim

JB284
Gold Trim

JB361
Gold Trim

JB377
Gold Trim

JB228
Gold Trim

JB510
Gold Trim

JB383
Platinum Trim

JB184
Gold Trim

JB10
Gold Trim

(Scalloped) JB-3 Shape

JB488
Gold Trim

JB211
Gold Trim

JB293
Gold Trim

JB633
Gold Trim

JB438
Gold Trim

JB34
Gold Trim

JB58
Gold Trim

JB437
Gold Trim

JB450
Gold Trim

JB-3 Shape (Scalloped)

JB43
Gold Trim

JB365
Gold Trim

JB273
Gold Trim

JB691
Gold Trim

JB692
Gold Trim

JB550
Gold Trim

JB181
Gold Trim

Castle On The Lake–Brown/Multicolor
No Trim

(Scalloped) JB-8 Shape

JB168
White Body
No Trim

JB359
Platter Shown
Cream Body
No Trim

Goldendawn
No Trim

Rosedawn
No Trim

Greendawn
No Trim

Greydawn
No Trim

JB442
No Trim

JB35
No Trim

JB52
Luncheon Plate Shown
Platinum Trim

JB-8 Shape (Scalloped)

JB330
Salad Plate Shown
Gold Trim

JB49
Black Verge
Gold Trim

JB84
Gold Trim

JB101
No Trim

Clarissa
Saucer Shown
No Trim

JB320
Luncheon Plate Shown
Platinum Trim

JB218
Salad Plate Shown
Gold Trim

The Claridge
Gold Trim

JB576
Bread & Butter Plate Shown
Gold Trim

(Scalloped) JB-8 Shape

Plymouth
Gold Trim

Belgravia
Gold Trim

The Regent
Gold Trim

Harcourt
Gold Trim

The Gerrard
Gold Trim

Clayton
Bread & Butter Plate Shown
Gold Trim

Drayton
Gold Trim

JB254
Red Trim

The Langhorn
Gold Trim

21

JB-8 Shape (Scalloped)

Sweet Briar
Luncheon Plate Shown
Yellow Trim

Yale
Gold Trim

Victoria
Gold Trim

Coronado
Gold Trim

Riviera
Gold Trim

The Jewel
Gold Trim

The Cavendish
Luncheon Plate Shown
Gold Trim

Adam
Gold Trim

Acton
Gold Trim

(Scalloped) JB-8 Shape

Brittany
Mustard Trim

The Belvedere
Bread & Butter Plate Shown
Gold Trim

The Marquis
Gravy Boat Shown
Gold Trim

The Russell
Platter Shown
Gold Trim

Douglas
Gold Trim

Derwent
Gold Trim

Cardiff
Gold Trim

The Cambridge
Gold Trim

JB712
Cereal Bowl Shown
Gold Trim

23

JB-8 Shape (Scalloped)

Jasmine
Gold Trim

Acanthus
Gold Trim

The Lombardy
Gold Trim

The Monterey
Gold Trim

The Grafton
Gold Trim

Ontwood
Gold Trim

Veronese
Bread & Butter Plate Shown
Gold Trim

Wentworth
Luncheon Plate Shown
No Trim

Tulip Time–Blue
Blue Background
No Trim

(Scalloped) JB-8 Shape

Elizabeth–Blue
Blue Background
No Trim

Dover–Blue
No Trim

Dover–Mulberry
No Trim

Dover–Red
No Trim

Dover–Brown
No Trim

Dover–Multicolor
No Trim

London Shape (Scalloped)

London White
No Trim

Richmond Hill
No Trim

Bloomsbury
Salad Plate Shown
No Trim

Mayfair
Salad Plate Shown
No Trim

Park Lane
Salad Plate Shown
No Trim

Orchid Splendour
No Trim

Spring Impressions
No Trim

Tropicanna
No Trim

Hyde Park
No Trim

(Scalloped) Heirloom Shape

Provincial
No Trim

Blue Jardin
No Trim

Fleur L'Orange
No Trim

Country Clare
Brown Trim

Berries
Green Trim

Bonjour
Red Trim

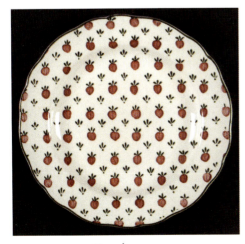
Bordeaux
Green Trim

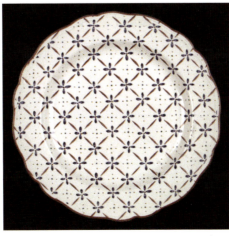
La Rochelle
Red Trim

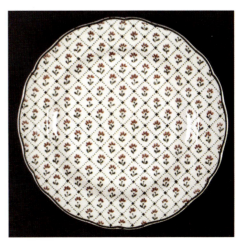
Montpellier
Green Trim

Heirloom Shape (Scalloped)

Monticello
Red Trim

Provincial pattern. Back Row: *Platter, Teapot with Lid.* Middle Row: *Round Covered Vegetable Bowl, Sugar Bowl with Lid, Creamer.* Front Row: *Salt & Pepper Set, Cereal Bowl, Cup & Saucer Set.*

(Scalloped) Elite Shape

JB163
Luncheon Plate Shown
No Trim

JB209
Round Covered Vegetable Bowl Shown
Gold Trim

JB588
Gold Trim

The Malvern
Gold Trim

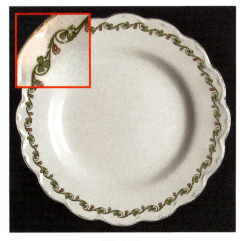

JB618
Gold Trim

JB481
Gold Trim

Ruth–Green
Gold Trim

Ruth–Blue/Green
Gold Trim

JB400
Gold Trim

Elite Shape (Scalloped)

JB364
Salad Plate Shown
Gold Trim

JB518
Soup Bowl Shown
Gold Trim

The Baroda
Gold Trim

JB38
No Trim

JB251
Bread & Butter Plate Shown
No Trim

JB409
Platter Shown
No Trim

JB257
No Trim

JB179
Luncheon Plate Shown
Gold Trim

The Balmoral
Gold Trim

(Scalloped) Elite Shape

The Simplon
Gold Trim

JB397
Gold Trim

Savoy
Salad Plate Shown
Flow Blue
Gold Trim

Savoy (Flow Blue) pattern. Tureen with Underplate, Pitcher.

Laurel Shape (Scalloped)

JB398
No Trim

JB159
Luncheon Plate Shown
No Trim

JB474
Gold Trim

Touraine
Gold Trim

The Regent
No Trim

JB123
Gold Trim

JB627
No Trim

JB358
No Trim

JB229
Gold Trim

(Scalloped) Laurel Shape

JB558
Oval Covered Vegetable Bowl Shown
Gold Trim

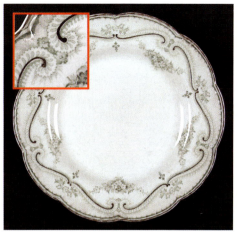
Regis–Green
Gold Trim

Regis–Blue
Luncheon Plate Shown
Gold Trim

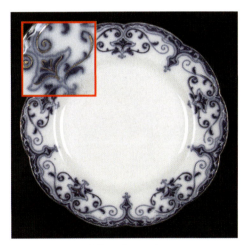
The Jewel
Flow Blue
Gold Trim

Newport
Green Ribbon
Gold Trim & Accents

Vintage
Blue Ivy
No Trim

Vintage
Blue/Green Ivy
Gold Trim

The Mikado–Green
Gold Trim

Normandy
Flow Blue
Gold Trim

Laurel Shape (Scalloped)

Holland
Flow Blue
Blue Trim

Normandy (Flow Blue) pattern. Left to Right: Cereal Bowl, Gravy Boat, Soup Bowl with Rim, Fruit Bowl.

Normandy (Flow Blue) pattern. Back Row: Dinner Plate, Oval Platter. Front Row: Oval Vegetable Bowl, Fruit Bowl, Cereal Bowl, Cup & Saucer Set.

(Scalloped) JB-12 Shape

JB133
Luncheon Plate Shown
No Trim

JB270
Gold Trim

Chantilly Gold
Gold Trim

JB314
Salad Plate Shown
Gold Bands
No Trim

JB269
No Trim

JB106
Cereal Bowl Shown
Gold Band
No Trim

JB54
Saucer Shown
Gold Trim

JB460
Gravy Boat Shown
No Trim

JB231
Gold Band
No Trim

JB-10 Shape (Scalloped)

JB408
Luncheon Plate Shown
No Trim

JB601
Gold Trim

JB428
Gold Trim

Beaufort
Gold Trim & Accents

Andorra
Chop Plate Shown
Flow Blue
No Trim

Andorra
Flow Blue
Gold Trim & Accents

Tokio
Flow Blue
Gold Trim & Accents

Oxford
Flow Blue
Gold Trim & Accents

(Scalloped) St. Elmo Shape

JB253
Saucer Shown
Gold Trim

JB131
No Trim

JB650
No Trim

The Tuscany
Gold Trim

JB681
Gold Trim

Delmonte
Creamer Shown
Flow Blue
No Trim

Delmonte
Platter Shown
Flow Blue
Gold Trim & Accents

The Lothair
Green/Gray Flowers
No Trim

The Lothair
Blue Flowers
Gold Trim & Accents

St. Elmo Shape (Scalloped)

Sanoma
Gold Trim

Marlboro–Blue
Gold Trim & Accents

Marlboro–Green
Gold Trim & Accents

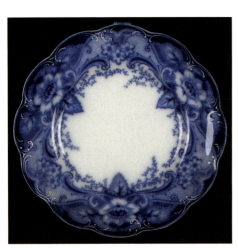

Argyle–Blue
Flow Blue
No Trim

The Lothair (Gold Trim & Accents) pattern. Top Row Above: Luncheon Plate, Oval Platter. Middle Row Above: Cup & Saucer Set (Oversized), Round Covered Butter Dish. Front Row Above: Demitasse Cup & Saucer Set, Cup & Saucer Set, Butter Pat. Left: Tureen with Lid.

(Scalloped) JB-11 Shape

JB216
Platinum Trim

JB571
Butter Pat Shown
Gold Trim

JB391
Gold Trim

JB403
Luncheon Plate Shown
Gold Trim

JB496
Soup Bowl Shown
Gold Trim

JB-15 Shape (Scalloped)

JB111
Salad Plate Shown
No Trim

JB598
Gold Trim

JB246
Salad Plate Shown
No Trim

JB355
No Trim

Dresden
No Trim

Dresdon–Flow Blue
Luncheon Plate Shown
No Trim

Prince
Saucer Shown
No Trim

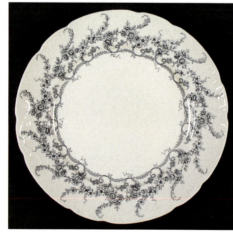

Venice–Blue/Gray
No Trim

Venice–Flow Blue
Gold Trim

(Scalloped) JB-15 Shape

Peach–Flow Blue
Saucer Shown
Gold Accents
No Trim

Tulip
Platter Shown
Flow Blue
No Trim

Clarissa
Gravy Boat Shown
Flow Blue
No Trim

Begonia–Blue
Saucer Shown
Gold Trim

41

JB-16 Shape (Scalloped)

JB524
Gold Trim

JB604
No Trim

JB444
No Trim

JB511
Platter Shown
Gold Trim

Neapolitan–Brown
Luncheon Plate Shown
No Trim

Neapolitan–Green
Oval Covered Vegetable Bowl Shown
No Trim

Neapolitan–Flow Blue
No Trim

Neapolitan–Flow Blue
Luncheon Plate Shown
Gold Accents
No Trim

Neapolitan–Blue
Luncheon Plate Shown
Gold Trim

(Scalloped) JB-16 Shape

Savoy
No Trim

Savoy–Flow Blue
Luncheon Plate Shown
No Trim

Neapolitan (Flow Blue, Gold Accents) pattern. Left to Right: *Gravy Boat with Underplate, Oval Platter, Fruit Bowl, Butter Pat.*

JB-18 Shape (Scalloped)

JB178
Luncheon Plate Shown
No Trim

JB463
Salad Plate Shown
No Trim

JB388
No Trim

JB421
No Trim

JB291
Luncheon Plate Shown
No Trim

JB544
No Trim

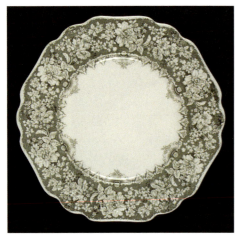

Havana
Luncheon Plate Shown
No Trim

Cloverly–Green
No Trim

Cloverly–Green
Gold Accents
No Trim

(Scalloped) JB-18 Shape

Cloverly–Green
Platter Shown
Gold Trim

Cloverly–Green
Gold Trim & Accents

Cloverly–Green (with pink roses)
Butter Pat Shown
Gold Trim

Cloverly–Blue/Green
Fruit Bowl Shown
No Trim

Cloverly–Blue
No Trim

Cloverly–Blue
Gold Trim & Accents

Claremont
Flow Blue
No Trim

Brooklyn
Luncheon Plate Shown
Flow Blue
No Trim

Florida
Flow Blue
No Trim

JB-20 Shape (Scalloped)

Clarissa–Green
Gold Trim & Accents

Savannah–Green
Salad Plate Shown
Gold Trim & Accents

Savannah–Purple
Salad Plate Shown
No Trim

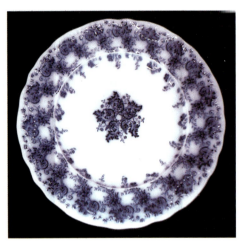

Fortuna
Flow Blue
No Trim

Albany
Flow Blue
Gold Trim & Accents

Albany
Cup & Saucer Set Shown
Flow Blue
No Trim

Astoria
Gravy Boat Shown
Flow Blue
Gold Trim

(Scalloped) Erminie Shape

JB347
No Trim

JB652
No Trim

JB108
Gold Trim

JB250
No Trim

JB230
No Trim

JB313
Salad Plate Shown
No Trim

JB669
No Trim

Dorothy
Gold Trim

Dorothy
No Trim

Erminie Shape (Scalloped)

Dorothy
Gravy Boat Shown
Flow Blue
No Trim

Montana–Flow Blue
No Trim

Montana–Green
Gold Trim

St. Louis
Flow Blue
Gold Trim

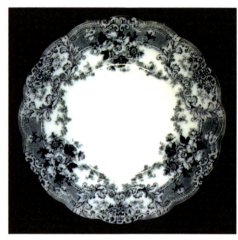
Venetian–Blue/Green
No Trim

The Florentine–Green
Gold Trim & Accents

Regent–Aqua
Luncheon Plate Shown
Gold Accents
No Trim

Regent–Flow Blue
Salad Plate Shown
Gold Trim

Regent–Flow Blue
Gold Trim & Verge

(Scalloped) Silver Shape

JB93
No Trim

JB190
Gold Trim & Design

JB523
Gold Trim & Design

JB369
No Trim

The Bergen Rose
No Trim

JB69
No Trim

JB670
No Trim

JB124
No Trim

JB586
Salad Plate Shown
No Trim

49

Silver Shape (Scalloped)

JB433
No Trim

Rolland–Green
Gold Trim

Rolland–Blue/Green
Gold Trim

JB499
Salad Plate Shown
No Trim

Wild Rose
Gold Trim & Accents

Dartmouth–Green
Gold Trim & Accents

Dartmouth–Blue
Flow Blue
No Trim

Eclipse
Gold Trim & Accents

Coral
Flow Blue
Gold Trim

(Scalloped) Silver Shape

Kenworth
Flow Blue
No Trim

Oregon
Relish/Gravy Underplate Shown
Flow Blue
No Trim

Oregon
Flow Blue
Gold Trim & Accents

The Blue Danube
Flow Blue
Gold Trim

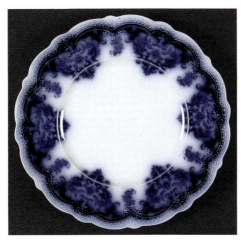

Georgia
Flow Blue
No Trim

Georgia
Flow Blue
Gold Trim & Accents

JB-21 Shape (Scalloped)

JB232
Luncheon Plate Shown
No Trim

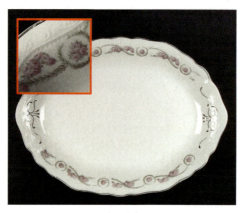

JB337
Platter Shown
Gold Trim

JB592
No Trim

JB684
Luncheon Plate Shown
No Trim

JB626
Luncheon Plate Shown
No Trim

JB23
Luncheon Plate Shown
No Trim

JB307
No Trim

The Madrid
Gold Trim

Worcester
Gold Trim & Accents

(Scalloped) JB-21 Shape

Glenwood–Green
Luncheon Plate Shown
Gold Trim

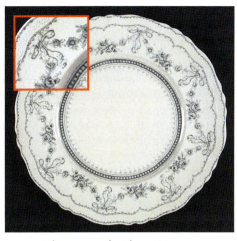

Glenwood–Blue/Green
No Trim

Glenwood–Blue/Green
Platter Shown
Gold Trim & Accents

Glenwood–Flow Blue
Oval Vegetable Bowl Shown
Gold Trim & Accents

Glenwood–Flow Blue
No Trim

Persian
Flow Blue
No Trim

Pekin
Flow Blue
No Trim

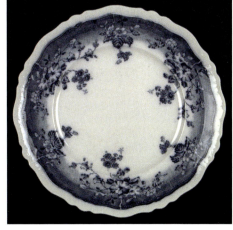

Clayton–Flow Blue
No Trim

Clayton–Flow Blue
Gravy Boat Shown
Gold Trim

JB-21 Shape (Scalloped)

Clayton–Blue Transferware
Oval Covered Vegetable Bowl Shown
No Trim

Clayton–Blue Transferware
Soup Bowl Shown
Gold Trim

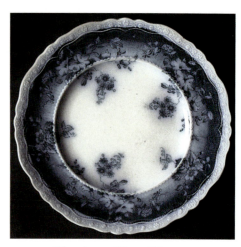

Clayton–Blue/Green
Bread & Butter Plate Shown
No Trim

Glenwood–Green pattern. **Back Row:** *Oval Platter, Luncheon Plate.* **Middle Row:** *Oval Covered Vegetable Bowl, Round Covered Vegetable Bowl.* **Front Row:** *Cup & Saucer Set, Butter Pat, Sugar Bowl with Lid, Fruit Bowl.*

(Scalloped) Old English Shape

JB305
No Trim

Belmont
Gold Bands
Gold Trim

JB503
Gold Bands
Gold Trim

JB140
Blue & Gold Bands
Gold Trim

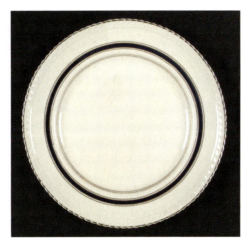

JB387
Cobalt & Gold Bands
Gold Trim

JB352
Taupe Band
No Trim

JB620
Green Band
No Trim

JB589
Aqua Band
No Trim

Powder Border
Green Speckled Band
No Trim

Old English Shape (Scalloped)

JB404
Platter Shown
Orange & Gold Bands
No Trim

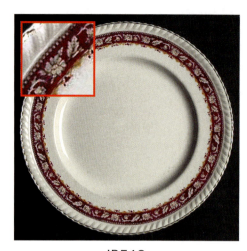

JB519
Red Band, White Flowers
Gold Trim

JB83
Blue Band
Gold Trim

JB47
Red Band
No Trim

Maldon
Gold Trim

Guildford–Maroon
Gold Trim

JB137
Gold Trim

Norton
Gold Trim

Belvedere
Gold Trim

(Scalloped) Old English Shape

JB420
Gold Trim

Eastbourne
Gold Trim

Kent
Gold Trim

Harrow
Gold Trim

JB94
No Trim

JB255
Gold Trim

Hampton
Gold Trim

JB553
Platter Shown
Gold Trim

JB227
Gold Trim

57

Old English Shape (Scalloped)

JB733
Bread & Butter Plate Shown
Gold Trim

JB100
Salad Plate Shown
Gold Trim

JB636
Gold Trim

JB686
Gold Trim

JB531
No Trim

Devonshire–Blue
No Trim

Devonshire–Green
No Trim

Devonshire–Brown/Multicolor
No Trim

Devonshire–Red/Multicolor
No Trim

(Scalloped) Old English Shape

Devonshire–Red
No Trim

Margaret Rose–Pink/Multicolor
No Trim

Margaret Rose–Brown/Multicolor
No Trim

Margaret Rose–Green/Multicolor
No Trim

Empire Grape
No Trim

Clover Time–Green
No Trim

Clover Time–Blue
No Trim

JB138
Gold Trim

Prince Of Wales
No Trim

Old English Shape (Scalloped)

JB4
Blue Band
No Trim

JB117
Maroon Band
No Trim

Ranelagh
Blue Band
No Trim

JB335
Saucer Shown
Blue Band
No Trim

JB21
Different Color Borders
No Trim

JB19
No Trim

JB18
No Trim

JB1
Multi-Motif (Different Color
Borders & Center Scenes)
No Trim

JB210
Salad Plate Shown
Blue Band
No Trim

(Scalloped) Old English Shape

JB516
Green Band
No Trim

JB33
Gold Band
No Trim

JB334
Maroon Band
Gold Trim

JB249
Blue Band
Gold Trim

JB169
Blue Band
Gold Trim

JB430
Red Band
No Trim

JB439
Maroon Bands
No Trim

Chadwell
Blue Bands
No Trim

JB662
Blue Bands
No Trim

61

Old English Shape (Scalloped)

JB425
Blue Bands
No Trim

Belford
No Trim

Winchester–Pink
No Trim

The Vigo
Gold Trim

Queen's Bouquet
Gold Trim

JB486
Yellow Trim

JB66
Gold Trim

JB534
No Trim

JB696
Gold Trim

(Scalloped) Old English Shape

JB556
Gold Trim

English Rose
Gold Trim

Rambler Rose
No Trim

JB136
Gold Trim

JB256
Gold Trim

JB583
Bread & Butter Plate Shown
Gold Trim

JB568
Salad Plate Shown
Gold Trim

JB453
Gold Trim

The Marquis
No Trim

Old English Shape (Scalloped)

Appleblossom–Pink
No Trim

Appleblossom–Brown/Multicolor
No Trim

Appleblossom–Dark Gray/Black
No Trim

Appleblossom–Green
No Trim

Appleblossom–Blue
No Trim

Castle On The Lake–Pink/Red
No Trim

Castle On The Lake–Brown/Multicolor
No Trim

Castle On The Lake–Blue
No Trim

Old Flower Prints
Multi-Motif
No Trim

(Scalloped) Old English Shape

Garden Bouquet
No Trim

Pomona
No Trim

Bird Of Paradise
165522
No Trim

English Bouquet
No Trim

Barnyard King
No Trim

JB212
Gold Trim

Old English Scalloped Shape (Scalloped)

Old English–White
No Trim

Fleurette
Red Trim

Vintage
No Trim

Garden Party
No Trim

Additional pieces in the Garden Party pattern. Back Row: *Round Vegetable Bowl, Oval Platter, Coffeepot with Lid.* Front Row: *Cup & Saucer Set, Teapot with Lid, Sugar Bowl with Lid, Creamer.*

(Scalloped) JB-6 Shape

JB353
Saucer Shown
No Trim

JB252
No Trim

JB575
No Trim

Edgvale–Green
Soup Bowl Shown
No Trim

Edgvale–Blue/Green
Bone Dish Shown
No Trim

Waverley
Platter Shown
No Trim

JB147
No Trim

JB578
Gold Trim

Raleigh
Salad Plate Shown
No Trim

JB-6 Shape (Scalloped)

Raleigh
Gold Trim

Richmond
Dessert Plate Shown
Flow Blue
No Trim

Stanley
Saucer Shown
Flow Blue
Gold Accents, No Trim

JB147 pattern. Back Row: *Oval Platter, Dinner Plate.* Middle Row: *Round Covered Butter Dish, Creamer, Oval Covered Vegetable Bowl.* Front Row: *Fruit Bowl, Butter Pat, Cup & Saucer Set.*

(Scalloped) Old Staffordshire Shape

Old Staffordshire–White
No Trim

Rosedawn
No Trim

Old Staffordshire–Pink
No Trim

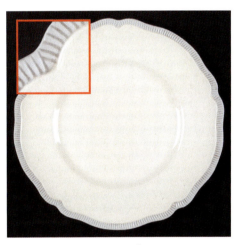
JB207–Blue
Salad Plate Shown
No Trim

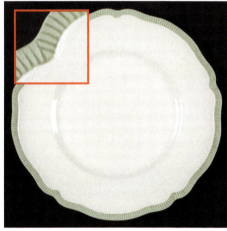
JB207–Green
Salad Plate Shown
No Trim

JB697
No Trim

Marseilles
Gold Trim

Greenway
Gold Trim

Malvern
Older
Gold Trim

Old Staffordshire Shape (Scalloped)

Hanford
Gold Trim

Ilford
Gold Trim

Meadowsweet
Gold Trim

Ningpo
Gold Trim

Kildare
Gold Trim

Lichfield
Gold Trim

Carlton
Gold Trim

Granville
Gold Trim

Moorland
Yellow Trim

(Scalloped) Old Staffordshire Shape

JB606
Gold Trim

Summer
Gold Trim

English Bouquet
No Trim

Dorchester
No Trim

Persian Tulip–Mulberry/Multicolor
Platter Shown
No Trim

Persian Tulip–Blue
No Trim

Chatsworth
Gold Trim

English Gardens–Blue
Luncheon Plate Shown
Multi-Motif
No Trim

English Gardens–Brown
Multi-Motif
No Trim

Old Staffordshire Shape (Scalloped)

English Gardens–Green
Multi-Motif
No Trim

Italian Lakes
Salad Plate Shown
No Trim

Old Britain Castles–Pink
Cereal Bowl Shown
No Trim

Persian Tulip–Blue pattern. Back Row Above: *Oval Platter, Dinner Plate.* Front Row Above: *Cup & Saucer Set, Cream Soup Bowl, Lugged Fruit Bowl, Sugar Bowl with Lid, Creamer.* Right: *Fruit Bowl, Soup Bowl, Soup Bowl with Rim.*

(Scalloped) Old Staffordshire 1 Shape

JB72
Salad Plate Shown
No Trim

JB161
Mustard Trim

JB536
Green Trim

Norwood
Brown Trim

Bordeaux–Brown
Bread & Butter Plate Shown
Brown Trim

JB339
No Trim

Marlow
Mustard Trim

Melbourne
Brown Trim

Dubarry
Tan Trim

Old Staffordshire 1 Shape (Scalloped)

Rouen
Mustard Trim

The Lucerne
Mustard Trim

Century Of Progress
Multi-Motif
No Trim

Dubarry pattern. Back Row: *Oval Platter.* Middle Row: *Creamer, Gravy Boat with Attached Underplate, Sugar Bowl with Lid, Round Vegetable Bowl.* Front Row: *Fruit Bowl, Cup & Saucer Set.*

(Scalloped) Old Staffordshire 2 Shape

JB285
Bread & Butter Plate Shown
No Trim

JB728
Bread & Butter Plate Shown
No Trim

Old Staffordshire 3 Shape (Scalloped)

JB718
White Background
No Trim

JB73
Cream Background
No Trim

JB713
Multi-Motif
No Trim

JB418
No Trim

JB593
No Trim

JB399
Gold Trim

JB475
No Trim

JB67
No Trim

Garden Bouquet
No Trim

(Scalloped) Old Staffordshire 3 Shape

Old English Chintz–Lavender/Multicolor
No Trim

Old English Chintz–Blue/Multicolor
No Trim

JB73 pattern. Demitasse Cup & Saucer Set, Cup & Saucer Set.

Richmond Shape (Scalloped)

Richmond White
No Trim

Caroline
No Trim

Orchard
Red Trim

Springfield
No Trim

Additional pieces in the Richmond White pattern. Back Row Above: Oval Platter. Middle Row Above: Square Salad Plate, Sugar Bowl with Lid, Coffeepot with Lid. Front Row Above: Creamer, Cup & Saucer Set, Teapot with Lid. Left: Tureen with Lid, Salt & Pepper Set, Round Covered Vegetable Bowl.

(Scalloped) Georgian Shape

Inverness
No Trim

Warwick–Pink
No Trim

Warwick–Mulberry
No Trim

Warwick–Brown/Multicolor
No Trim

Oriental Rose–Brown
No Trim

Maydelle–Green
Salad Plate Shown
No Trim

JB9
No Trim

Windsor Flowers
No Trim

Wakefield
No Trim

Georgian Shape (Scalloped)

Malvern–Red
No Trim

Malvern–Plum
No Trim

Malvern–Blue
No Trim

Malvern–Brown/Multicolor
No Trim

Windsor Fruit
No Trim

Mount Vernon–Pink
Multi-Motif
No Trim

Mount Vernon–Blue
Multi-Motif
No Trim

Mount Vernon–Green/Multicolor
Multi-Motif
No Trim

Mount Vernon–Brown/Multicolor
Multi-Motif
No Trim

(Scalloped) Georgian Shape

Azalea Gardens
Multi-Motif
No Trim

Malvern–Blue pattern. Left to Right: *Soup Bowl with Rim, Round Vegetable Bowl, Cereal Bowl, Fruit Bowl.*

Malvern–Blue pattern. Back Row: *Gravy Boat with Attached Underplate, Oval Platter, Round Covered Vegetable Bowl.* Front Row: *Creamer, Cup & Saucer Set, Fruit Bowl.*

81

Sovereign Shape (Scalloped)

Sovereign
No Trim

Brookshire
Green Trim

Enfield
Gold Trim

JB60
Gold Trim

Connaught
Gold Trim

Romance
Gold Trim

JB447
Mustard Trim

Guernsey
Gold Trim

Malaga
Gold Trim

(Scalloped) Sovereign Shape

Sicily
Gold Trim

Ellastone
Gold Trim

Ravary
Luncheon Plate Shown
Gold Trim

Springtime
Gold Trim

Glencoe
Gold Trim

Lenora
Bread & Butter Plate Shown
Yellow Trim

Duchess
Gold Trim

JB342
Luncheon Plate Shown
Gold Trim

Rutland
Gold Trim
(The flat pieces in this pattern are square shapes, but the hollowware pieces match other Sovereign hollowware shapes.)

Sovereign Shape (Scalloped)

Buttercup
No Trim

JB515
Green Trim

JB260
Gold Trim

Otley
Bread & Butter Plate Shown
No Trim

Hydrangea Blue
Blue Trim

Lynton
Newer
No Trim

Princess Mary
Mustard Trim

JB505
Gold Trim

JB435
Bread & Butter Plate Shown
Gold Trim

(Scalloped) Sovereign Shape

JB642
No Trim

JB86
Mustard Trim

JB572
Green Trim

JB489
Green Trim

JB621
Gold Trim

Princess
Gold Trim

Bird Of Paradise
No Trim

Apple Harvest
No Trim

The Road Home
No Trim

Sovereign Shape (Scalloped)

Royal Homes Of Britain–Blue
Multi-Motif
No Trim

Royal Homes Of Britain–Red
Soup Bowl Shown
Multi-Motif
No Trim

Haddon Hall–Pink
No Trim

Haddon Hall–Brown/Multicolor
No Trim

Haddon Hall–Blue
No Trim

Old Britain Castles–Pink
Multi-Motif
No Trim

Old Britain Castles–Blue
Multi-Motif
No Trim

Old Britain Castles–Green
Multi-Motif
No Trim

Old Britain Castles–Black
Multi-Motif
No Trim

(Scalloped) Sovereign Shape

Old Britain Castles–Brown
Multi-Motif
No Trim

Old Britain Castles–Brown/Multicolor
Multi-Motif
No Trim

Old Britain Castles–Lavender
Multi-Motif
No Trim

Old Britain Castles–Pink (Christmas)
Multi-Motif
No Trim

Old London–Blue
Multi-Motif
No Trim

Old London–Brown/Multicolor
Multi-Motif
No Trim

Castle Story–Blue
Multi-Motif
No Trim

Castle Story–Pink
Multi-Motif
No Trim

Old English Countryside–Pink
No Trim

Sovereign Shape (Scalloped)

Old English Countryside–Green
No Trim

Old English Countryside–Blue
Bread & Butter Plate Shown
No Trim

Old English Countryside–Brown
No Trim

Old English Countryside–Brown/Multicolor
No Trim

Road to Windsor–Red
No Trim

Enchanted Garden–Pink
No Trim

Enchanted Garden–Blue
No Trim

Enchanted Garden–Plum
No Trim

Enchanted Garden–Brown/Multicolor
No Trim

(Scalloped) Sovereign Shape

English Chippendale–Red
No Trim

English Chippendale–Blue
No Trim

English Chippendale–Green
No Trim

English Countryside–Pink/Multicolor
No Trim

Old English Chintz–Pink
Chop Plate Shown
No Trim

Old English Chintz–Blue
No Trim

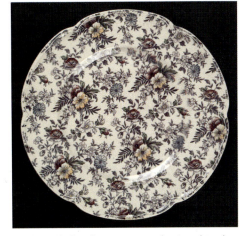
Old English Chintz–Lavender/Multicolor
No Trim

Old English Chintz–Blue/Multicolor
Bread & Butter Plate Shown
No Trim

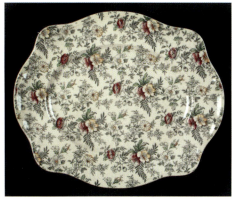
Old English Chintz–Green/Multicolor
Platter Shown
No Trim

Sovereign Shape (Scalloped)

Old English Chintz–Pink/Multicolor
No Trim

Old Britain Castles–Pink pattern. Tureen with Lid, Canisters.

Old Britain Castles–Pink pattern. Back Row: *Oval Platter, Dinner Plate, Coffeepot with Lid.* Middle Row: *Pitcher, Rice Bowl Mini, Teapot with Lid, Eggcup, Sugar Bowl with Lid.* Front Row: *Breakfast Cup & Saucer Set, Cup & Saucer Set, Creamer.*

(Scalloped) Old Chelsea Shape

JB31
Gold Trim

Vintage
No Trim

Strawberry Fair
No Trim

JB128
Gold Trim

JB392
Bread & Butter Plate Shown
Gold Trim

JB271
Gold Trim

JB664
Gold Trim

JB65
Gold Trim

JB483
Gold Trim

Old Chelsea Shape (Scalloped)

JB327
Platter Shown
Gold Trim

JB381
Gold Trim

JB451
Gold Trim

JB214
Gold Trim

JB641
Gold Trim

Day In June–Burgundy
No Trim

Day In June–Green
No Trim

Day In June–Multicolor
No Trim

Elizabeth–Pink
No Trim

(Scalloped) Old Chelsea Shape

Elizabeth–Mulberry
No Trim

Elizabeth–Brown
No Trim

Elizabeth–Blue
No Trim

Sheraton
No Trim

Rose Chintz–Pink
No Trim

Rose Chintz–Blue
No Trim

Susanna
Multi-Motif
Brown Trim

Harvest Time–Blue
No Trim

Harvest Time–Brown/Multicolor
No Trim

93

Old Chelsea Shape (Scalloped)

Georgia–Multicolor
No Trim

Windsor Fruit
No Trim

Autumn's Delight
No Trim

The Old Mill–Brown/Multicolor
No Trim

The Old Mill–Brown
No Trim

The Old Mill–Pink
No Trim

The Old Mill–Purple
No Trim

The Old Mill–Blue
No Trim

Pastorale Toile De Jouy–Green
No Trim

(Scalloped) Old Chelsea Shape

Pastorale Toile De Jouy–Pink
No Trim

Pastorale Toile De Jouy–Plum
No Trim

Pastorale Toile De Jouy–Brown
No Trim

Pastorale Toile De Jouy–Brown/Multicolor
No Trim

Happy England–Green/Multicolor
No Trim

Millstream–Blue
No Trim

Millstream–Pink
No Trim

Millstream–Brown/Multicolor
No Trim

Country Life
No Trim

Old Chelsea Shape (Scalloped)

Tally Ho
No Trim

The Friendly Village
Multi-Motif
No Trim

The Friendly Village–Christmas
No Trim

Merry Christmas
No Trim

Additional pieces in The Friendly Village pattern. Back Row Left: *Oval Turkey Platter.* Middle Row Left: *Goblet, Double Old Fashioned Glassware, Metal Kettle.* Front Row Left: *Cheese Plane, Pie Server.*

Additional pieces in The Friendly Village pattern. Back Row Below: *Two Oval Platters.* Front Row Below: *Spoon Rest, Utensil Holder, Covered Casserole.*

His Majesty
No Trim

(Scalloped) Regency Shape

Regency
Ironstone
No Trim

Canterbury
Bone China
No Trim

Dreamland
Blue Trim

JB673
Platinum Trim

JB498
Gold Trim

JB513
Platter Shown
Platinum Trim

JB504–Scalloped
Platter Shown
Gold Trim

Minuet
No Trim

Encore
No Trim

Regency Shape (Scalloped)

Melody
Blue Trim

Thistle
Green Trim

Summer Chintz
Red Trim

JB309
Platinum Trim

Cottage Garden
Platter Shown
Gold Trim

Cherry Blossom
Green Trim

English Rose
Green Trim

Fairwood
No Trim

Dolores
Platinum Trim

(Scalloped) Regency Shape

Strawberry Fayre
Round Vegetable Bowl Shown
No Trim

Charlotte
No Trim

Marlow
Newer
No Trim

JB671
Gold Trim

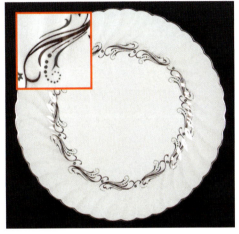
Venetian
R12664
Gold Trim

JB605
Gold Trim

JB482
Salad Plate Shown
Platinum Trim

Kensington
No Trim

JB602
Platinum Trim

Regency Shape (Scalloped)

Lynmere
Gold Trim

Enchantment
Gold Trim

JB139
Platinum Trim

JB628
Platinum Trim

JB431
Salad Plate Shown
Platinum Trim

JB432
Gold Trim

JB695
Square Salad Plate Shown
Multi-Motif
Platinum Trim

Staffordshire Bouquet
No Trim

Devon Sprays–Brown/Multicolor
No Trim

(Scalloped) Regency Shape

Devon Sprays–Pink
No Trim

Devon Sprays–Blue
No Trim

Indies–Blue
No Trim

Indies–Pink
No Trim

Indies–Green
Bread & Butter Plate Shown
No Trim

Rose Bouquet–Blue
No Trim

Rose Bouquet–Pink
No Trim

JB370
Bread & Butter Plate Shown
No Trim

Jolie–Pink/Multicolor
No Trim

Regency Shape (Scalloped)

Rose Garden
Salad Plate Shown
Pink Trim

Sweetbriar
Red Trim

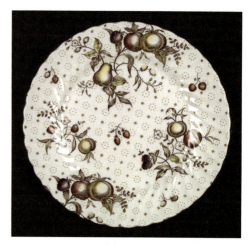
Eddington
No Trim

Summer Chintz (All Over Design)
Red Trim

Bradbury–Red
No Trim

Old Bradbury–Pink
No Trim

These patterns appear to be the same, but are marked using a different name.

Bradbury–Blue
No Trim

Old Bradbury–Blue
White Background
No Trim

Old Bradbury–Blue
Cream Background
No Trim

These patterns appear to be the same, but are marked using a different name.

(Scalloped) Regency Shape

Liberty–Blue
No Trim

Lotus–Blue
No Trim

Lotus–Red/Pink
No Trim

Paisley–Red
No Trim

Paisley–Brown
No Trim

Paisley–Green
No Trim

Paisley–Black
No Trim

Saxony
No Trim

Blue Nordic
No Trim

Regency Shape (Scalloped)

Tulip Time–Brown/Multicolor
No Trim

Tulip Time–Blue
No Trim

Heritage Hall–Blue
4411
Multi-Motif
No Trim

Heritage Hall–Brown/Multicolor
4411
Multi-Motif
No Trim

Royal Homes Of Britain–Red
No Trim

English Country Life
Multi-Motif
No Trim

Coaching Scenes–Brown/Multicolor
No Trim

Coaching Scenes–Pink
No Trim

Coaching Scenes–Green
Teapot Shown
No Trim

(Scalloped) Regency Shape

Coaching Scenes–Blue
No Trim

Happy England–Blue
No Trim

Happy England–Red/Pink
No Trim

Spring
No Trim

Ancient Towers–Brown/Multicolor
Sandwich Tray Shown
No Trim

Ancient Towers–Pink
Cream Soup Cup & Saucer Set Shown
No Trim

Cotswold–Blue
No Trim

Cotswold–Pink
No Trim

Cotswold–Brown
No Trim

Regency Shape (Scalloped)

Watermill–Brown
No Trim

JB603
Square Salad Plate Shown
No Trim

Coaching Scenes–Blue pattern. Back Row: *Dinner Plate, Oval Platter,* Front Row: *Cup & Saucer Set, Teapot with Lid, Mini Teapot with Lid, Round Covered Vegetable Bowl.*

(Scalloped) JB-28 Shape

JB14
Gold Trim

Stanhope
Yellow Trim

JB261
Blue Trim

Horton
Platter Shown
Blue Trim

JB585
Platter Shown
Rust Trim

Stafford
Blue Trim

The Mayfair
Salad Plate Shown
Mustard Trim

Burton
Luncheon Plate Shown
Gold Trim

JB206
Blue Trim

107

JB-28 Shape (Scalloped)

Eden
Bread & Butter Plate Shown
Yellow Trim

Alton
Gold Trim

The Ellerton
Salad Plate Shown
Blue Trim

Albany
Yellow Trim

Geneva
Mustard Trim

Newark
Bread & Butter Plate Shown
Blue Trim

JB413
Blue Trim

JB414
Gold Trim

JB720
Saucer Shown
Gold Trim

(Scalloped) Heritage Shape

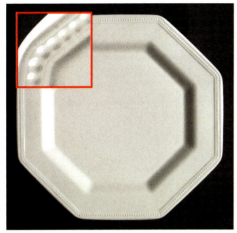

Heritage–White
No Trim

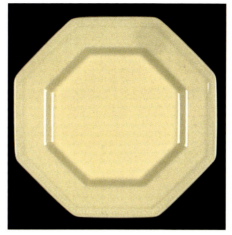

Heritage–Yellow
No Trim

Posy
No Trim

Revere
No Trim

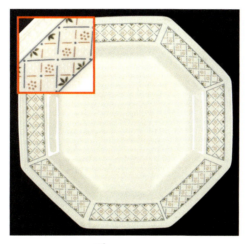

Chequers
No Trim

Madison
Red Trim

Eternal Belle
Green Trim

Eternal Beau
Green Trim

Enchantment
Red Trim

Heritage Shape (Scalloped)

Sandringham
Green Trim

Spring Morning
No Trim

Sonata
Platter Shown
Green Trim

Elegance
No Trim

JB351
Platter Shown
Green Trim

Greenfield
No Trim

Lemon Tree
No Trim

Persian Garden
No Trim

Ming
No Trim

(Scalloped) Heritage Shape

Jacobean
No Trim

Hyde Park–Blue
No Trim

Hyde Park–Brown
No Trim

Fresh Fruit
Green Trim

Heritage–Yellow pattern (above). Back Row: *Oval Covered Vegetable Bowl, Oval Platter, Sugar Bowl with Lid, Creamer.* Front Row: *Salt & Pepper Set, Cup & Saucer Set, Gravy Boat.*

Additional pieces in the Fresh Fruit pattern (left). Left to Right: *Tureen with Lid, Oval Platter, Creamer, Salad Plate, Sugar Bowl with Lid, Cup & Saucer Set.*

111

JB-27 Shape (Scalloped)

JB103
No Verge
Gold Trim

JB32
Gold Trim & Verge

JB378
Gold Trim

The Arno
Gold Trim

JB175
Bread & Butter Plate Shown
Gold Trim

JB197
Gold Trim

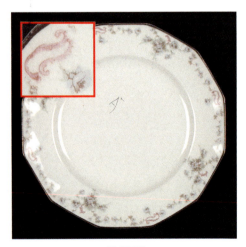

JB276
Salad Plate Shown
Gold Trim

JB105
Salad Plate Shown
Gold Trim

Royston
Luncheon Plate Shown
Flow Blue
Gold Trim

(Scalloped) JB-27 Shape

Kenworth
Flow Blue
No Trim

JB215
Salad Plate Shown
Gold Trim

JB135
Gold Trim

JB494
Gold Trim

Fushan
Thin Gold Verge
Gold Trim

JB132
Wide Gold Verge
Gold Trim

JB441
Salad Plate Shown
Green Trim & Verge

JB729
Green Trim

113

Miscellaneous Scalloped Rim Shapes

JB304
Platter Shown
No Trim

JB306
JB-14 Shape
No Trim

JB658
Luncheon Plate Shown
JB-19 Shape
No Trim

JB68
JB-17 Shape
No Trim

JB203
Gravy Boat Shown
Gold Trim

JB449
Salad Plate Shown
No Trim

JB295
Bread & Butter Plate Shown
No Trim

JB680
Tureen Shown
Gold Trim

JB412
Cake Plate Shown
Gold Trim

Miscellaneous Scalloped Rim Shapes

Woodland
Covered Vegetable Bowl Shown
No Trim

Arcadia
Multi-Motif
Green Trim

Peach Bloom
Brown Trim

JB497
No Trim

Waldorf
Luncheon Plate Shown
No Trim

Windsor
Luncheon Plate Shown
Gold Trim

Savoy–Multicolor
Newer
Gray Trim

Sheringham
No Trim

Asiatic Pheasants–Pink
No Trim

Miscellaneous Scalloped Rim Shapes

Asiatic Pheasants–Blue
No Trim

Asiatic Pheasants–Black
No Trim

Fruit Basket Green
Roman Shape
No Trim

(Smooth) Athena Shape

Athena
No Trim

Embassy
No Trim

JB323
Platinum Trim

JB324
Platter Shown
Platinum Trim

Scandia
No Trim

JB380
Blue Trim

Silhouette
No Trim

Arcadia
No Trim

Plum Blossom
No Trim

Athena Shape (Smooth)

Deauville
No Trim

Athena pattern (above). Back Row: *Coffeepot with Lid, Teapot with Lid, Pitcher.* Front Row: *Tureen with Lid, Salt & Pepper Set, Round Covered Vegetable Bowl.*

Athena pattern (above). Left to Right: *Oval Covered Casserole, Rice Bowl, Round Covered Vegetable Bowl, Fruit Bowl, Ramekin.*

Athena pattern (right). Back Row: *Gravy Boat with Underplate, Oval Platter, Sugar Bowl with Lid, Creamer.* Front Row: *Fruit Bowl, Cup & Saucer Set, Ramekin, Demitasse Cup & Saucer Set.*

(Smooth) JB-26 Shape

Delhi
Red Trim

JB492
Gold Trim

JB263
Saucer Shown
Gold Trim

Edward
Gold Trim

JB527
No Trim

Vincent
Dessert Plate Shown
Gold Trim

Constance
Luncheon Plate Shown
Gold Trim

JB411
Gold Trim

JB177
Gold Trim

JB-26 Shape (Smooth)

JB659
No Trim

Constance pattern. Back Row: *Round Covered Vegetable Bowl, Oval Platter, Cranberry Bowl.* Front Row: *Creamer, Cup & Saucer Set, Fruit Bowl.*

(Floral, Middle Design, Gold Trim) Miscellaneous Smooth Rim Shapes

JB322
Salad Plate Shown

JB455
Luncheon Plate Shown

JB362
Luncheon Plate Shown

JB427

JB461

JB753
Salad Plate Shown

Celestial

JB318
Bread & Butter Plate Shown

JB243
Green Band

Miscellaneous Smooth Rim Shapes (Floral, Middle Design, Gold Trim)

JB46
Aqua Band

Vogue
Older

Villa

Marjorie
No Verge

Minorca
Gold Verge

JB454
Salad Plate Shown

JB385
Salad Plate Shown

JB82

JB424

(Floral, Middle Design, Gold Trim) Miscellaneous Smooth Rim Shapes

Sultana

Petroushka

Arcadian

Scarabee

Mongolia

The Madras

JB59

JB39
Luncheon Plate Shown

Reliance

Miscellaneous Smooth Rim Shapes (Floral, Middle Design, Gold Trim)

Fantasio

JB338

Beauvais

JB90

St. Cloud

JB654

JB495

JB162

The Vigo

(Floral, Middle Design, Gold Trim) Miscellaneous Smooth Rim Shapes

JB477
Soup Bowl Shown

Paradise

Paradise

Mayfair

Balmoral

JB287

Satsouma

Tokio–Blue/Gray

Tokio–Flow Blue

Miscellaneous Smooth Rim Shapes (Floral, Middle Design, Gold Trim)

Marlborough

JB13

JB711
Green Rim

JB41
Blue Band

JB42
Blue Band

JB114
Blue Band

JB311
Maroon Band

JB145
Wide Maroon Band

JB724
Thin Maroon Band

(Floral, Middle Design, Gold Trim) Miscellaneous Smooth Rim Shapes

JB477
Soup Bowl Shown

Paradise

Paradise

Mayfair

Balmoral

JB287

Satsouma

Tokio–Blue/Gray

Tokio–Flow Blue

Miscellaneous Smooth Rim Shapes (Floral, Middle Design, Gold Trim)

Marlborough

JB13

JB711
Green Rim

JB41
Blue Band

JB42
Blue Band

JB114
Blue Band

JB311
Maroon Band

JB145
Wide Maroon Band

JB724
Thin Maroon Band

126

(Floral, Middle Design, Gold Trim) Miscellaneous Smooth Rim Shapes

JB325
Green Band

JB708
Green Band

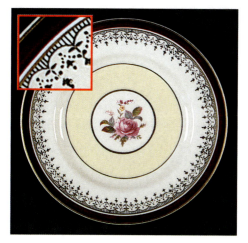

JB201
Bread & Butter Plate Shown
Maroon Band

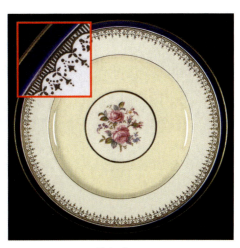

Frinton
Blue Band

Miscellaneous Smooth Rim Shapes (Floral, No Middle Design, Gold Trim)

JB44

JB220

JB265
Soup Bowl Shown

JB332

Hevella

JB56

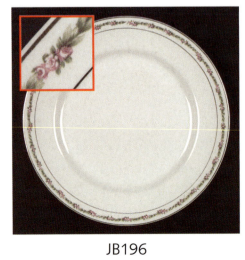
JB196

JB185

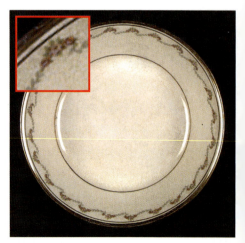
JB24

(Floral, No Middle Design, Gold Trim) Miscellaneous Smooth Rim Shapes

JB213

The Orkney

JB45

JB205

JB416
Saucer Shown

JB174

JB17

JB752
No Verge

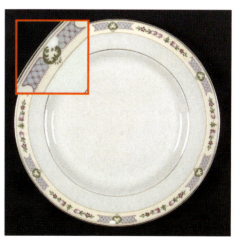
JB57
Gold Verge

129

Miscellaneous Smooth Rim Shapes (Floral, No Middle Design, Gold Trim)

JB345

JB657

JB50
Bread & Butter Plate Shown

JB522
Fruit Bowl Shown

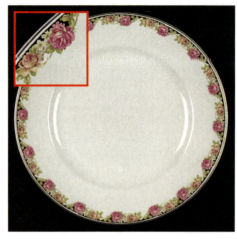
JB233

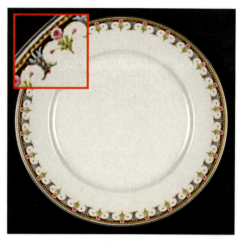
JB171

JB735

JB281

JB574
Platter Shown

(Floral, No Middle Design, Gold Trim) Miscellaneous Smooth Rim Shapes

JB134
Platter Shown

JB122
Luncheon Plate Shown

Bagatelle

JB71

JB170

Dudley

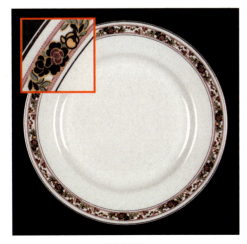

JB303

JB288

JB493

Miscellaneous Smooth Rim Shapes (Floral, No Middle Design, Gold Trim)

JB29

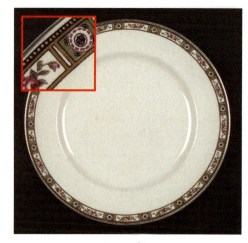
Ormsby

JB130

JB545

Montrose
Luncheon Plate Shown

Oakworth

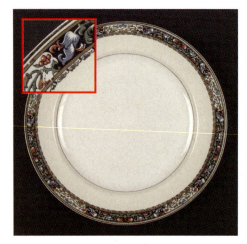
Granada

JB457

JB118
Bread & Butter Plate Shown

(Floral, No Middle Design, Gold Trim) Miscellaneous Smooth Rim Shapes

JB78

JB102

Seville

Rita

JB7
Luncheon Plate Shown

JB264
Salad Plate Shown

Netherland
Bread & Butter Plate Shown

JB535
Round Covered Vegetable Bowl Shown

JB92

133

Miscellaneous Smooth Rim Shapes (Floral, No Middle Design, Gold Trim)

Devon

JB565
Bread & Butter Plate Shown

JB172

Chester

Melba
Luncheon Plate Shown

JB749

JB348

JB121

JB119

(Floral, No Middle Design, Gold Trim) Miscellaneous Smooth Rim Shapes

Sheraton

JB16

JB183

JB30

JB126

The Bombay

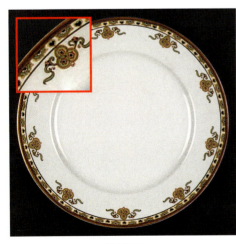

JB552

JB539

JB167

Miscellaneous Smooth Rim Shapes (Floral, No Middle Design, Gold Trim)

JB582

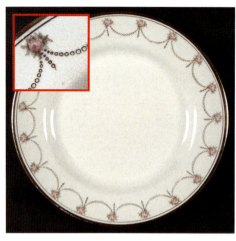

JB104
Salad Plate Shown

JB504–Smooth
Platter Shown

JB709
Fruit Bowl Shown

JB374

JB195
Platter Shown

JB452

JB730

JB543

(Floral, No Middle Design, Gold Trim) Miscellaneous Smooth Rim Shapes

Poppy

Rossmore

Ashville

Shalford

Redditch

Redcliffe

JB219

Square Salad Plate Shown
(Dinner Plates in this pattern are smooth.)

Watteau
Tan Scrolls & Dots Border

Watteau
Yellow Ovals Border

137

Miscellaneous Smooth Rim Shapes (Floral, No Middle Design, Gold Trim)

Miami

Lorraine

Eastbourne

JB521

JB579
Luncheon Plate Shown

Adam

JB25
Bread & Butter Plate Shown

The Tarifa
Platter Shown

JB329

(Floral, No Middle Design, Gold Trim) Miscellaneous Smooth Rim Shapes

Twyford

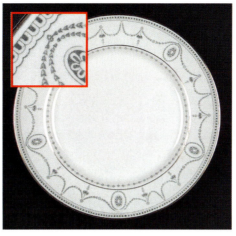
Sultana–Blue/Green

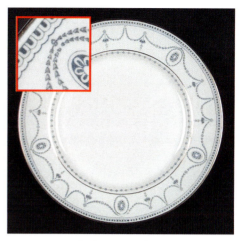
Sultana–Blue

Haverhill

JB189–Cream
Cream Background
No Verge

JB189
Luncheon Plate Shown
White Background
No Verge

JB537
Salad Plate Shown
Gold Verge

JB366

Netherlands

Miscellaneous Smooth Rim Shapes (Floral, No Middle Design, Gold Trim)

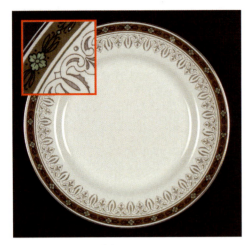

Verona
Salad Plate Shown

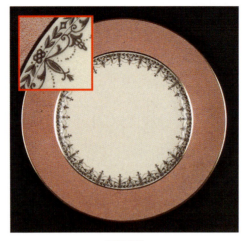

JB298
Luncheon Plate Shown

JB382

JB597
Salad Plate Shown

JB193
Saucer Shown

Washington
CS104-62

Lyric

Bradford

Matlock

(Floral, No Middle Design, Gold Trim) Miscellaneous Smooth Rim Shapes

Lorna

Belgravia

JB458

Lindsey

Chester–Blue

Chester–Green
Platter Shown

Kashan
Saucer Shown

JB470
Soup Bowl Shown

Nassau
Luncheon Plate Shown

141

Miscellaneous Smooth Rim Shapes (Floral, No Middle Design, Gold Trim)

JB434

JB528

JB647

Henley–Pink

Henley–Green
Salad Plate Shown

Henley–Blue

Turin–Blue
Flow Blue

142

(Non-Floral, Gold Trim) Miscellaneous Smooth Rim Shapes

The Grosvenor

Westbourne

JB235

JB570
Soup Bowl Shown
One Black Band

Raleigh
Two Black Bands

JB546
Platter Shown
Blue Band

JB36
Salad Plate Shown
No Verge
Blue Band

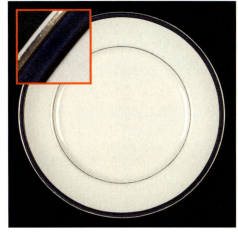

JB112
Gold Verge
Blue Band

JB89
Blue Band

Miscellaneous Smooth Rim Shapes (Non-Floral, Gold Trim)

Goldein
No Verge

Claridge
Salad Plate Shown
Gold Verge

JB410
No Verge

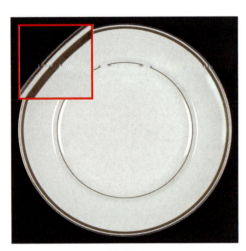

JB631
Gold Verge

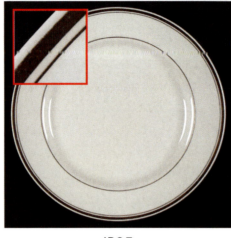

JB95
Luncheon Plate Shown

JB37

JB109

JB99
Fruit Bowl Shown

JB301

(Non-Floral, Gold Trim) Miscellaneous Smooth Rim Shapes

JB415

JB350

JB191

JB144
Bread & Butter Plate Shown

JB239
Cream Soup & Saucer Set Shown
Gray Band

JB316
Salad Plate Shown
Maroon Band

JB286
Platter Shown
Red Band

JB645
Green Bands

JB422
Demitasse Saucer Shown
Orange Bands

Miscellaneous Smooth Rim Shapes (Non-Floral, Gold Trim)

JB151
Salad Plate Shown

JB225
Light Yellow Band

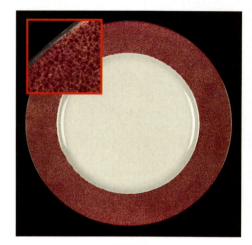

JB716
Red Speckled Band

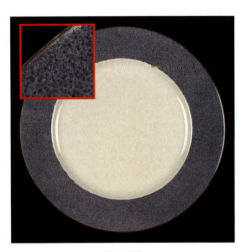

JB150
Blue Speckled Band

JB20
Blue Band

JB732

Interlude

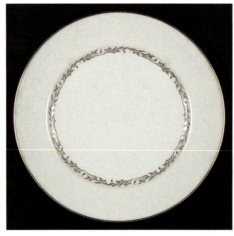

JB473

Whitehall
Green Band

(Non-Floral, Gold Trim) Miscellaneous Smooth Rim Shapes

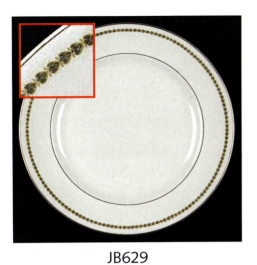
JB629

JB343
Saucer Shown

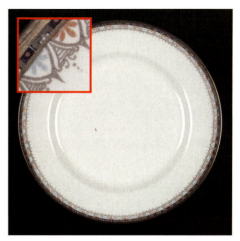
JB426

JB156

JB173

Blackwood

JB155
Luncheon Plate Shown

Bermuda

Algiers
Salad Plate Shown

Miscellaneous Smooth Rim Shapes (Non-Floral, Gold Trim)

JB326

Senora–Green
Round Covered Vegetable Bowl Shown

Senora–Blue

Medici–Gold
Bread & Butter Plate Shown

Medici–Black

Medici–Red
Cereal Bowl Shown

The Pontracina

The Trieste
Flow Blue

(Platinum or Other Trim) Miscellaneous Smooth Rim Shapes

Desert Sand
Brown Trim

Carlyle
Platinum Trim

JB372
Platinum Trim

Pirouette
Platinum Trim

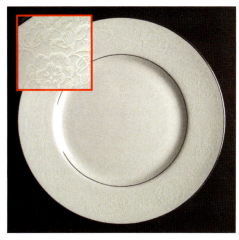
Organdy
Platinum Trim

Candlelight
Platinum Trim

Cameo
Platinum Trim

Erindale
Fruit Bowl Shown
Platinum Trim

JB357
Platinum Trim

Miscellaneous Smooth Rim Shapes (Platinum or Other Trim)

JB328
Platinum Trim

JB91
Bread & Butter Plate Shown
Platinum Trim

Ashley
Platinum Trim

JB462
Bread & Butter Plate Shown
Platinum Trim

Autumn Song
Platinum Trim

JB619
Platinum Trim

Lynton
Older
Platinum Trim

Sylvan
Platinum Trim

JB667
Bread & Butter Plate Shown
Platinum Trim

(Platinum or Other Trim) Miscellaneous Smooth Rim Shapes

JB164
Platinum Trim

Mitsouko
Red Trim

Chamonix
Yellow Trim

JB278
Saucer Shown
Mustard Trim

Ramsey
Green Trim

JB595
Cream Soup & Saucer Set Shown
Black Trim

Wild Flowers
Multi-Motif
Green Trim

Diamond Flowers
Green Trim

Spring Medley
Red Trim

Miscellaneous Smooth Rim Shapes (Platinum or Other Trim)

JB142
Saucer Shown
Green Band
Platinum Trim

JB63
Blue Rim
Platinum Trim

JB349
Luncheon Plate Shown
Light Green Rim
Platinum Trim

Everglade
Green Trim

Blue Savanna
Multi-Motif
Gray Trim

Paper Leaves
Multi-Motif
Green Trim

Sloane Square
Brown Trim

Malvern
Newer
Red Trim

Caribbean
Multi-Motif
Black Trim

(Platinum or Other Trim) Miscellaneous Smooth Rim Shapes

JB204
Salad Plate Shown
Platinum Trim

JB81
Platinum Trim

Staffordshire Gardens
Salad Plate Shown
Multi-Motif
Green Trim

Meadow Lane
Green Trim

Misty Morning
Green Trim

Spring Day
Yellow Trim

Straw Hat
Brown Trim

Honey Bunch
Brown Trim

Fancy Free
Brown Trim

Miscellaneous Smooth Rim Shapes (Platinum or Other Trim)

Cheyne Walk
Brown Trim

King's Road
Green Trim

Pimlico
Brown Trim

JB541
Mustard Trim

Ballad
Platinum Trim

Wildflowers
Pink Trim

JB198
Yellow Trim

Arundale
Orange Trim

Meadow Brook
Multi-Motif
Green Trim

(Platinum or Other Trim) Miscellaneous Smooth Rim Shapes

Fruit Sampler
Newer
Multi-Motif
Brown Trim

JB64
Salad Plate Shown
Mustard Trim

Lincoln
Orange Trim

Jefferson
Orange Trim

Mayflower
Mustard Trim

Garfield
Mustard Trim

Columbus
Mustard Trim

Madison
Mustard Trim

JB685
Mustard Trim

Miscellaneous Smooth Rim Shapes (Platinum or Other Trim)

JB107
Platinum Trim

JB116
Platinum Trim

JB321
Luncheon Plate Shown
Platinum Trim

JB614
Salad Plate Shown
Platinum Trim

JB148
Platinum Trim

JB182
Bread & Butter Plate Shown
Platinum Trim

Brighton
Platinum Trim

(No Trim) Miscellaneous Smooth Rim Shapes

JB509

Apollo
Apollo Shape

Roulette
Roulette Shape

Colonial
Colonial Shape

Classic White
Classic Shape

JB563
Soup Bowl Shown
Celadon Body

JB308
Light Blue Body

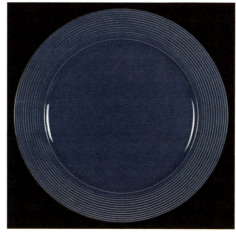
Chargers (Service Plates)
Various Colors

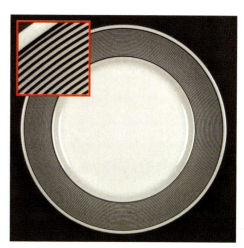
Orbit

Miscellaneous Smooth Rim Shapes (No Trim)

Fjord

Creme Caramel

English Oak

Auburn

Summerfields

Wild Cherries

Impact

Panache

Tracy

(No Trim) Miscellaneous Smooth Rim Shapes

Lucerne

Summer Delight
Green Band

JB125
Luncheon Plate Shown

JB559
Bouillon Cup & Saucer Set Shown

Delamere

Retford

Old English Trellis

Country Craft
Red Band

JB540
Fruit Bowl Shown

Miscellaneous Smooth Rim Shapes (No Trim)

The Villiers

Davenport
Luncheon Plate Shown

Haverhill

The Pontracina

Ashford Blue

Stratford Pink

Harwood Mulberry

Sheldon Charcoal

Portland
Multi-Motif

(No Trim) Miscellaneous Smooth Rim Shapes

Juliette
Multi-Motif

Katherine

JB336

Cornflower

Windfall
Multi-Motif

Waterfall

Ice Blue
Multi-Motif

The Trieste
Flow Blue

Glendevon

Miscellaneous Smooth Rim Shapes (No Trim)

Springfield
Multi-Motif

Medina
Multi-Motif

Papyrus
Multi-Motif

McBaine
Multi-Motif

Manorwood
Multi-Motif

Enchanted Garden
Multi-Motif

Acanthus Cream
Multi-Motif

Acanthus Blue
Multi-Motif

River Scenes
Multi-Motif

(No Trim) Miscellaneous Smooth Rim Shapes

Kew Gardens

Strawberry Fields

Somerton

Golden Pears
Multi-Motif

Autumn Grove

Tea Leaf
Copper Band & Design

Herbs
Salad Plate Shown
Multi-Motif

JB459
Cereal Bowl Shown
Green Band

Cerise

Miscellaneous Smooth Rim Shapes (No Trim)

Jardiniere–Green

Jardiniere–Yellow

Seaside
Multi-Motif

The Exeter

Old English Clover–Brown

Old English Clover–Pink
Platter Shown

Lace–Gray
Older

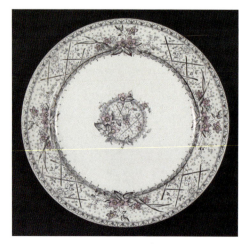
Lace–Pink
Older

Amsterdam

(No Trim) Miscellaneous Smooth Rim Shapes

Quadrille

Tudor Flowers

Kristina

Brandywine

Victorian Christmas
Multi-Motif

Twelve Days Of Christmas
Multi-Motif

Denmark–Pink

Denmark–Black

Denmark–Blue

Miscellaneous Smooth Rim Shapes (No Trim)

Tokio
Oval Vegetable Bowl Shown
Flow Blue

Kyoto

Ancient Towers–Blue
Breakfast Cup & Saucer Set Shown

JB472

Indian Tree
Brown Greek Key

Indian Tree
White Background
Green Greek Key

Indian Tree
Cream Background
Green Greek Key

JB146
Beige Greek Key

Chloe

166

(No Trim) Miscellaneous Smooth Rim Shapes

Gingham

Winchester
Saucer Shown

Patchwork Farm

Mongolia–Flow Blue

Mongolia–Blue/Gray

Blue Tapestry

Chelsea Rose
Multi-Motif

Butterfly
Salad Plate Shown

Tiffany Menagerie
Multi-Motif

Miscellaneous Smooth Rim Shapes (No Trim)

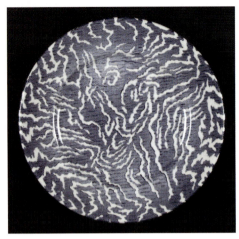
English Oak

Hunam–Blue

Neighbors
Multi-Motif

Historic America–Brown/Multicolor
Multi-Motif

Historic America II–Brown
Multi-Motif

Historic America–Blue
Multi-Motif

Historic America–Pink
Multi-Motif

Willow–Pink/Red

Willow–Blue

(No Trim) Miscellaneous Smooth Rim Shapes

JB640

Denmark–Blue pattern. Back Row: *Round Covered Vegetable Bowl, Oval Platter, Teapot with Lid.* Front Row: *Creamer, Cup & Saucer Set.*

Willow–Blue pattern. Back Row: *Oval Platter.* Middle Row: *Canister, Round Covered Casserole, Coffeepot with Lid.* Front Row: *Sugar Bowl with Lid, Creamer, Salt & Pepper Set, Teapot with Lid.*

Old Granite Shape (Coupe)

Cottage
No Trim

Lancaster
No Trim

Gretchen–Green
No Trim

Gretchen–Blue
No Trim

Danube
No Trim

Zephyr
Rust Trim

Orchard
No Trim

Provence
No Trim

Sun Up
No Trim

(Coupe) Old Granite Shape

Salem
No Trim

Fruit Sampler
Older
Multi-Motif
No Trim

Arbor
No Trim

Jamestown–Blue
White Background
No Trim

Jamestown–Blue
Tan Background
No Trim

Jamestown–Brown
No Trim

Cherry Thieves
No Trim

Hearts & Flowers
No Trim

Sugar & Spice–Blue
4413
No Trim

Old Granite Shape (Coupe)

Sugar & Spice–Brown
4413
No Trim

Petite Fleur–Blue
No Trim

Petite Fleur–Burgundy/Pink
No Trim

Oriental Garden
No Trim

Hearts & Flowers pattern. **Back Row Above:** *Coffeepot with Lid, Dinner Plate, Oval Platter, Round Covered Vegetable Bowl.* **Front Row Above:** *Cup & Saucer Set, Teapot with Lid, Sugar Bowl with Lid, Creamer.* **Left:** *Gravy Boat with Underplate, Mug, Salt & Pepper Set, Fruit Bowl.*

(Coupe) Focus Shape

Focus–White
No Trim

Blue Ice
No Trim

Early Dawn
No Trim

Vogue
No Trim

Celebrity
No Trim

Additional pieces in the Blue Ice pattern. Back Row: *Round Covered Vegetable Bowl, Oval Platter, Teapot with Lid.* Front Row: *Sugar Bowl with Lid, Fruit Bowl, Creamer, Gravy Boat.*

JB-9 Shape (Coupe)

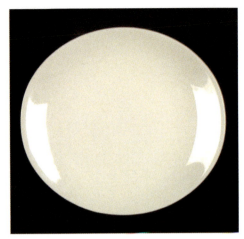

JB80
Bread & Butter Plate Shown
Cream Background
No Trim

Rose Cloud
Pink Background
No Trim

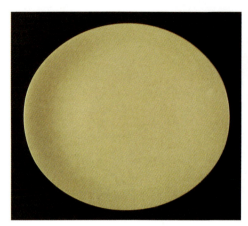

Golden Cloud
Yellow Background
No Trim

Green Cloud
Green Background
No Trim

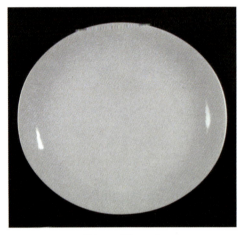

Blue Cloud
Blue Background
No Trim

JB238
Platinum Trim

Shower Of Roses
No Trim

JB746
No Trim

JB143
No Trim

(Coupe) JB-9 Shape

JB371
Gold Trim

JB517
Salad Plate Shown
No Trim

Game Birds
Multi-Motif
No Trim

Romance Of The Sea
No Trim

Seafare
Multi-Motif
No Trim

Fish
Multi-Motif
No Trim

Snow Crystals–Pink
No Trim

Lace–Pink
No Trim

Lace–Gray & Pink
No Trim

JB-9 Shape (Coupe)

Titania–Blue
No Trim

Glenwood
No Trim

Floating Leaves–Gray
No Trim

Floating Leaves–Pink
No Trim

Floating Leaves–Green
No Trim

JB743
No Trim

Dream Town–Green/Multicolor
No Trim

English Gardens–Green/Multicolor
No Trim

(Floral) Miscellaneous Coupe Shapes

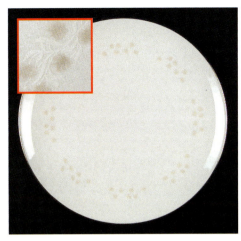
Beatrice
Platinum Trim

Flair
No Trim

Provincial
No Trim

Dutch Treat
No Trim

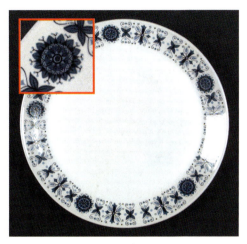
Engadine
No Trim

Sonoma
No Trim

JB402
Bread & Butter Plate Shown
No Trim

JB567
No Trim

Meadowbrook
No Trim

Miscellaneous Coupe Shapes (Floral)

Hopscotch–Blue
Multi-Motif
No Trim

Hopscotch–Red
No Trim

Nicole
No Trim

JB502
No Trim

JB141
Platinum Trim

JB419
Gold Trim

Only A Rose
No Trim

JB226
No Trim

JB617
No Trim

(Floral) Miscellaneous Coupe Shapes

JB340
No Trim

JB292
No Trim

JB479
No Trim

JB445
No Trim

Cambridge
Platinum Trim

JB560
Platter Shown
No Trim

JB443
No Trim

Autumn Mist
No Trim

JB490
Bread & Butter Plate Shown
No Trim

Miscellaneous Coupe Shapes (Floral)

JB508
Salad Plate Shown
No Trim

Barbados
Bread & Butter Plate Shown
No Trim

JB611
Platinum Trim

JB406
Gold Trim

JB53
Platinum Trim

Sirocco
No Trim

Summertime
No Trim

Misty
No Trim

Collage
No Trim

(Floral) Miscellaneous Coupe Shapes

Gossamer
No Trim

Charleston Garden
No Trim

Strawmarket
No Trim

Eton
Blue Trim

JB608
Cereal Bowl Shown
Blue Band

JB386
Platter Shown
Platinum Trim

JB240
No Trim

JB241
No Trim

Wildmoor
No Trim

Miscellaneous Coupe Shapes (Floral)

JB346
No Trim

JB637
Orange Trim

Pasadena
No Trim

JB356
No Trim

Kerrydale
No Trim

Lausanne
No Trim

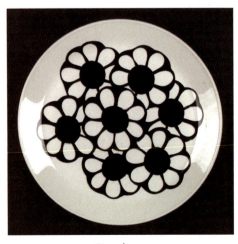
Cordova
No Trim

Samba
No Trim

Sierra
No Trim

(Floral) Miscellaneous Coupe Shapes

Camellia–Green
No Trim

Camellia–Pink
No Trim

Delray
No Trim

Monterey
No Trim

Carmel
No Trim

Marie
Blue Trim

Hampshire
No Trim

Azalea
No Trim

Romance
No Trim

Miscellaneous Coupe Shapes (Floral)

Springtime
Salad Plate Shown
No Trim

Holland–Blue
Multi-Motif
No Trim

Chanticleer–Brown
Saucer Shown
No Trim

Chanticleer–Blue
No Trim

Country Cupboard–Blue
No Trim

Country Cupboard–Brown
No Trim

(Non-Floral) Miscellaneous Coupe Shapes

JB423
No Trim

Tivoli–White
Tivoli Shape
No Trim

JB12
No Trim

Plaza
Platinum Trim

JB542
No Trim

JB487
Blue Background
No Trim

Patio–Blue
Blue Trim

Patio–Brown
Brown Trim

Simplicity–Red
Luncheon Plate Shown
Red Trim

Miscellaneous Coupe Shapes (Non-Floral)

Simplicity–Blue
Blue Trim

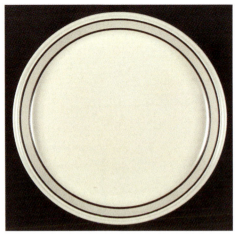
Sandlewood
No Trim

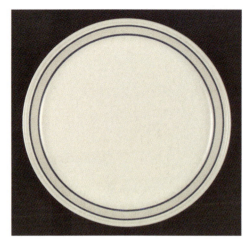
Finlandia–Blue
No Trim

Papaya
No Trim

Bahia
No Trim

Sierra
No Trim

JB157
No Trim

Malaga
No Trim

Lugano
No Trim

(Non-Floral) Miscellaneous Coupe Shapes

Louisiana
No Trim

JB395
No Trim

Fruit Cocktail
No Trim

Golden Apples
No Trim

Dorado
No Trim

Summer Gold
No Trim

Autumn Breezes
No Trim

Berry Branch
No Trim

JB79
No Trim

Miscellaneous Coupe Shapes (Non-Floral)

JB158
No Trim

JB533
No Trim

JB607
Gold Trim

Game Birds–Cream
Cream Background
Multi-Motif
No Trim

Game Birds–White
White Background
Multi-Motif
No Trim

Fish
Multi-Motif
No Trim

Conifer
Brown Trim

Wheat
Brown Trim

JB244
Salad Plate Shown
Multi-Motif
No Trim

(Non-Floral) Miscellaneous Coupe Shapes

Madrid
Cereal Bowl Shown
No Trim

Aurora
Salad Plate Shown
No Trim

Verona
No Trim

Sahara
Salad Plate Shown
No Trim

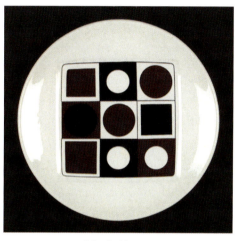
Variations
Bread & Butter Plate Shown
No Trim

Piazza
No Trim

Prado
No Trim

San Remo
No Trim

Dorado
No Trim

Miscellaneous Coupe Shapes (Non-Floral)

Rio Verde
No Trim

Snow Crystals–Blue
No Trim

Aquabatic
Multi-Motif
No Trim

Playtime
No Trim

Tower Bridge
No Trim

Windsor Castle
No Trim

Dream Town–Brown/Multicolor
No Trim

Multi-Motif Patterns

The Friendly Village

School House
Dinner Plate

Autumn Mists
Large Dinner Plate

Covered Bridge
Large Dinner Plate

Hayfield
Large Dinner Plate

Lily Pond
Large Dinner Plate

Old Mill
Large Dinner Plate

School House
Large Dinner Plate

Stone Wall
Large Dinner Plate

Sugar Maples
Large Dinner Plate

The Well
Large Dinner Plate

Village Green
Large Dinner Plate

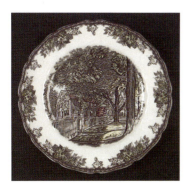
Village Street
Large Dinner Plate

Willow By The Brook
Large Dinner Plate

Turkey
Large Dinner Plate

Multi-Motif Patterns

Historic America II– Brown
(introduced in 2002)

Capital Building Washington, DC
Dinner Plate

Brooklyn Bridge
Accent Dinner Plate

Central Park Bethesda Fountain
Accent Dinner Plate

Empire State Building
Accent Dinner Plate

Statue Of Liberty
Accent Dinner Plate

The Flying Cloud
Accent Dinner Plate

Golden Gate Bridge
Accent Dinner Plate

The Mayflower
Accent Dinner Plate

Game Birds– White
(Round Shape)

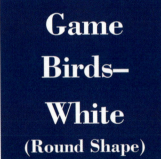
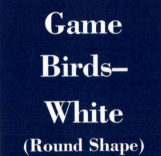
Partridge
Dinner Plate

Pheasant
Dinner Plate

Quail
Dinner Plate

Ruffed Grouse
Dinner Plate

Turkey
Dinner Plate

Woodcock
Dinner Plate

Multi-Motif Patterns

Game Birds– Cream
(Oval Shape)

Partridge
Dinner Plate

Pheasant
Dinner Plate

Quail
Dinner Plate

Ruffed Grouse
Dinner Plate

Turkey
Dinner Plate

Woodcock
Dinner Plate

Fish
(Oval Shape)

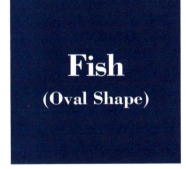
Dinner Plate

Dinner Plate

Dinner Plate

Dinner Plate

Dinner Plate

Dinner Plate

Dinner Plate

Multi-Motif Patterns

Seafare
(Oval Shape)

Cockle
Dinner Plate

Lobster
Dinner Plate

Mussel
Dinner Plate

Oyster
Dinner Plate

Twelve Days Of Christmas

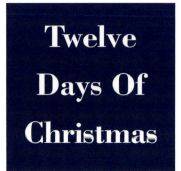

Partridge In A Pear Tree
Dinner Plate

Three French Hens
Dinner Plate

Five Golden Rings
Dinner Plate

Twelve Drummers
Dinner Plate

194

Johnson Brothers Backstamps

Shown below are a sampling of marks used by Johnson Brothers through the years. As can be seen, some marks indicate the pattern name, others the line, while many will only tell us that the product was made by Johnson Brothers in England.

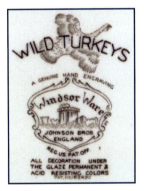

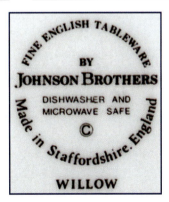

Index (A-D)

A

Acanthus 24
Acanthus Blue 162
Acanthus Cream 162
Acton 22
Adam (JB-8 Shape) 5, 22
Adam (Shape Unknown) 138
Albany 108
Albany (Flow Blue)
    Gold Trim & Accents 46
    No Trim 46
Alexander Pottery 4, 5
Algiers 147
Alton 108
Amsterdam 164
Ancient Towers (Regency Shape)
    Brown/Multicolor 105
    Pink 105
Ancient Towers (Shape Unknown)
    Blue 166
Andorra (Flow Blue)
    Gold Trim & Accents 36
    No Trim 36
Apollo 157
Apollo Shape 10, 157
Apple Harvest 85
Appleblossom–Blue 64
Appleblossom–Brown/Multicolor 64
Appleblossom–Dark Gray/Black 64
Appleblossom–Green 64
Appleblossom–Pink 64
Aquabatic 190
Arbor 171
Arcadia 115, 117
Arcadian 123
Argyle–Blue (Flow Blue) .... 38, Back Cover
Arno, The 112
Arundale 154
Ashford Blue 160
Ashley 150
Ashville 137
Asiatic Pheasants–Black 116
Asiatic Pheasants–Blue 116
Asiatic Pheasants–Pink 115
Astoria (Flow Blue) .... 46, Back Cover
Athena 117, 118
Athena (Viking) Shape 10, 117-118
Auburn 158
Aurora 189
Autumn Breezes 187
Autumn Grove 163
Autumn Mist 179
Autumn Song 150
Autumn's Delight 94
Azalea 183
Azalea Gardens 81

B

Bagatelle 131
Bahia 186
Ballad 154
Balmoral 125
Balmoral, The 30
Barbados 180
Barnyard King 65
Baroda, The 30
Beatrice 177
Beaufort 36
Beauvais 124
Begonia–Blue 41
Belford 62
Belgravia (JB-8 Shape) 21
Belgravia (Shape Unknown) 141
Belmont 55
Belvedere 56
Belvedere, The 23
Bergen Rose, The 49
Bermuda 147
Berries 27
Berry Branch 187
Bird Of Paradise 85
Bird Of Paradise 165522 65
Blackwood 147
Bloomsbury 26
Blue Cloud 174
Blue Danube, The (Flow Blue) ... 51, Back Cover
Blue Ice 173
Blue Jardin 27
Blue Nordic 103
Blue Savanna 152
Blue Tapestry 167
Bombay, The 135
Bonjour 27
Bordeaux 27
Bordeaux–Brown 73
Bradbury–Blue 102
Bradbury–Red 102
Bradford 140
Brandywine 165
Brighton 156
Brittany 23
Brooklyn (Flow Blue) 45
Brookshire 82
Burton 107
Buttercup 84
Butterfly 167

C

Cambridge 179
Cambridge, The 23
Camellia–Green 183
Camellia–Pink 183
Cameo 149
Candlelight 149
Canterbury 97
Cardiff 23
Caribbean 152
Carlton 70
Carlyle 149
Carmel 183
Caroline 78
Castle On The Lake (JB-3 Shape)
    Brown/Multicolor 18
Castle On The Lake (Old English Shape)
    Blue 64
    Brown/Multicolor 64
    Pink/Red 64
Castle Story–Blue 87
Castle Story–Pink 87
Cavendish, The 22
Celebrity 173
Celestial 121
Century Of Progress 74
Cerise 163
Chadwell 61
Charles Street Works 4
Chamonix 151
Chanticleer–Blue 184
Chanticleer–Brown 184
Chantilly Gold 35
Chargers (Service Plates) 157
Charleston Garden 181
Charlotte 99
Chatsworth 71
Chelsea Rose 167
Chequers 109
Cherry Blossom 98
Cherry Thieves 171
Chester–Blue 141
Chester–Green 141
Chester (Green Border) 134
Cheyne Walk 154
Chloe 166
Claremont (Flow Blue) .... 45, Front Cover
Claridge 144
Claridge, The 20
Clarissa (JB-8 Shape) 20
Clarissa (Flow Blue) (JB-15 Shape) 41
Clarissa–Green (JB-20 Shape) 46
Classic Shape 10, 157
Classic White 157
Clayton (JB-8 Shape) 21
Clayton (JB-21 Shape)
    Blue/Green 54
    Blue Transferware, Gold Trim 54
    Blue Transferware, No Trim 54
    Flow Blue, Gold Trim 53
    Flow Blue, No Trim 53
Clover Time–Blue 59
Clover Time–Green 59
Cloverly–Blue
    Gold Trim & Accents 45
    No Trim 45
Cloverly–Blue/Green 45
Cloverly–Green
    Gold Accents, No Trim 44
    Gold Trim & Accents 45
    Gold Trim 45
    No Trim 44
    with pink roses 45
Coaching Scenes–Blue 105, 106
Coaching Scenes–Brown/Multicolor ... 104
Coaching Scenes–Green 104
Coaching Scenes–Pink 104
Collage 180
Colonial 157
Colonial Shape 10, 157
Columbia 15
Columbus 155
Conifer 188
Connaught 82
Constance 119, 120
Convolvulus 14
Coral (Flow Blue) 50
Cordova 182
Cornflower 161
Coronado 22
Cotswold–Blue 105
Cotswold–Brown 105
Cotswold–Pink 105
Cottage 170
Cottage Garden 98
Country Clare 27
Country Craft 159
Country Cupboard–Blue 184
Country Cupboard–Brown 184
Country Life 95
Creme Caramel 158

D

Danube 170
Dartmouth–Blue (Flow Blue) 50
Dartmouth–Green 50
Davenport 160
Day In June–Burgundy 92
Day In June–Green 92
Day In June–Multicolor 92
Deauville 118
Delamere 159
Delhi 119
Delmonte (Flow Blue)
    Gold Trim & Accents 37
    No Trim 37

(D-H) Index

Delray ... 183
Denmark–Black ... 165
Denmark–Blue ... 165, 169
Denmark–Pink ... 165
Derwent ... 23
Desert Sand ... 149
Devon ... 134
Devon Sprays–Blue ... 101
Devon Sprays–Brown/Multicolor ... 100
Devon Sprays–Pink ... 101
Devonshire–Blue ... 58
Devonshire–Brown/Multicolor ... 58
Devonshire–Green ... 58
Devonshire–Red ... 59
Devonshire–Red/Multicolor ... 58
Diamond Flowers ... 151
Dolores ... 98
Dorado (Dark Beige & Orange) ... 189
Dorado (White with Fruit) ... 187
Dorchester ... 71
Dorothy (Flow Blue) ... 48
Dorothy (Gold Trim) ... 47
Dorothy (No Trim) ... 47
Douglas ... 23
Dover–Blue ... 25
Dover–Brown ... 25
Dover–Mulberry ... 25
Dover–Multicolor ... 25
Dover–Red ... 25
Drayton ... 21
Dream Town–Brown/Multicolor ... 190
Dream Town–Green/Multicolor ... 176
Dreamland ... 97
Dresden ... 40
Dresdon–Flow Blue ... 40
Dubarry ... 73, 74
Duchess ... 83
Dudley ... 131
Dutch Treat ... 177

E

Eagle Pottery ... 5
Early Dawn ... 173
Eastbourne (Old English Shape) ... 57
Eastbourne (Shape Unknown) ... 138
Eclipse ... 50
Eddington ... 102
Eden ... 108
Edgvale–Blue/Green ... 67
Edgvale–Green ... 67
Edward ... 119
Elegance ... 110
Elite Shape ... 6, 29-31
Elizabeth (JB-8 Shape)
  Blue ... 25
Elizabeth (Old Chelsea Shape)
  Blue ... 93
  Brown ... 93
  Mulberry ... 93
  Pink ... 92
Ellastone ... 83
Ellerton, The ... 108
Embassy ... 117
Empire Grape ... 59
Enchanted Garden (Shape Unknown) ... 162
Enchanted Garden (Sovereign Shape)
  Blue ... 88
  Brown/Multicolor ... 88
  Pink ... 88
  Plum ... 88
Enchantment (Heritage Shape) ... 109
Enchantment (Regency Shape) ... 100
Encore ... 97
Enfield ... 82
Engadine ... 177
English Bouquet (Old English Shape) ... 65
English Bouquet (Old Staffordshire Shape) ... 71
English Chippendale–Blue ... 89
English Chippendale–Green ... 89
English Chippendale–Red ... 89
English Country Life ... 104
English Countryside–Pink/Multicolor ... 89
English Gardens (JB-9 Shape, Oval)
  Green/Multicolor ... 176
English Gardens (Old Staffordshire Shape)
  Blue ... 71
  Brown ... 71
  Green ... 72
English Oak (Embossed Edge) ... 158
English Oak (Dark Blue & White) ... 168
English Rose (Old English Shape) ... 63
English Rose (Regency Shape) ... 98
Erindale ... 149
Erminie Shape ... 8, 47-48
Eternal Beau ... 109
Eternal Belle ... 109
Eton ... 181
Everglade ... 152
Exeter, The ... 164

F

Fairwood ... 98
Fancy Free ... 153
Fantasio ... 124
Finegan, Mary J. ... 5, 208
Finlandia–Blue ... 186
Fish (JB-9 Shape, Oval) ... 175, 193
Fish (Shape Unknown, Round) ... 188
Fjord ... 158
Flair ... 177
Fleur L'Orange ... 27
Fleurette ... 66
Floating Leaves–Gray ... 176
Floating Leaves–Green ... 176
Floating Leaves–Pink ... 176
Florentine–Green, The ... 48, Front Cover
Florida (Flow Blue) ... 45, Back Cover
Focus Shape ... 11, 173
Focus–White ... 173
Fortuna (Flow Blue) ... 46
Fresh Fruit ... 111
Friendly Village, The ... 96, 191
Friendly Village–Christmas, The ... 96
Frinton ... 127
Fruit Basket Green ... 116
Fruit Cocktail ... 187
Fruit Sampler (Newer) ... 155
Fruit Sampler (Older) ... 171
Fushan ... 113

G

Game Birds (JB-9 Shape, Oval) ... 175, 193
Game Birds (Shape Unknown, Round)
  Cream ... 188
  White ... 188, 192
Garden Bouquet (Old English Shape) ... 65
Garden Bouquet (Old Staffordshire 3 Shape) .. 76
Garden Party ... 66
Garfield ... 155
Geneva ... 108
Georgia (Flow Blue)
  Gold Trim & Accents ... 51
  No Trim ... 51
Georgia–Multicolor ... 94
Georgian Shape ... 9, 79-81
Gerrard, The ... 21
Gingham ... 167
Glencoe ... 83
Glendevon ... 161
Glenwood ... 176
Glenwood–Blue/Green
  Gold Trim & Accents ... 53
  No Trim ... 53
Glenwood–Flow Blue
  Gold Trim & Accents ... 53
  No Trim ... 53
Glenwood–Green ... 53, 54
Goldein ... 144
Golden Apples ... 187
Golden Cloud ... 174
Golden Pears ... 163
Goldendawn ... 19
Gossamer ... 181
Grafton, The ... 24
Granada ... 132
Granville ... 70
Green Cloud ... 174
Greendawn ... 19
Greenfield ... 110
Greenway ... 69
Gretchen–Blue ... 170
Gretchen–Green ... 170
Greydawn ... 4, 19
Grosvenor, The ... 143
Guernsey ... 82
Guildford–Maroon ... 56

H

Haddon Hall–Brown/Multicolor ... 86
Haddon Hall–Pink ... 86
Haddon Hall-Blue ... 86
Hampshire ... 183
Hampton ... 57
Hanford ... 70
Hanley ... 5
Hanley Pottery ... 4
Happy England (Old Chelsea Shape)
  Green/Multicolor ... 95
Happy England (Regency Shape)
  Blue ... 105
  Red/Pink ... 105
Hanley Pottery ... 4
Harcourt ... 21
Harrow ... 57
Harvest ... 13
Harvest Time–Blue ... 93
Harvest Time–Brown/Multicolor ... 93
Harwood Mulberry ... 160
Havana ... 44
Haverhill (Gold Trim) ... 139
Haverhill (No Trim) ... 160
Hearts & Flowers ... 171, 172
Heirloom Shape ... 6, 27-28
Henley–Blue ... 142
Henley–Green ... 142
Henley–Pink ... 142
Herbs ... 163
Heritage Hall–Blue 4411 ... 104
Heritage Hall–Brown/
  Multicolor 4411 ... 104, Front Cover
Heritage Shape ... 10, 109-111
Heritage–White ... 109
Heritage–Yellow ... 109, 111
Hevella ... 128
His Majesty ... 96, Front Cover
Historic America–Blue ... 168
Historic America–Brown/Multicolor ... 168
Historic America–Pink ... 168
Historic America II–Brown ... 168, 192
Holland (Flow Blue) ... 34
Holland–Blue ... 184
Honey Bunch ... 153
Hop ... 14
Hopscotch–Blue ... 178
Hopscotch–Red ... 178

Index (H-O)

Horton 107
Hunam–Blue 168
Hyde Park (Heritage Shape)
    Blue 111
    Brown 111
Hyde Park (London Shape) 26
Hydrangea Blue 84

I
Ice Blue 161
Ilford 70
Impact 158
Imperial Works Pottery 4
Indian Tree
    Brown Greek Key 166
    Cream Background, Green Greek Key 166
    White Background, Green Greek Key 166
Indies–Blue 101
Indies–Green 101
Indies–Pink 101
Interlude 146
Inverness 79
Italian Lakes 72

J
Jacobean 111
Jamestown–Blue
    Tan Background 171
    White Background 171
Jamestown–Brown 171
Jardiniere–Green 164
Jardiniere–Yellow 164
Jasmine 24
JB-2 Shape 6, 13
JB-3 Shape 6, 16-18
JB-5 Shape 6, 14-15
JB-6 Shape 8, 67-68
JB-8 Shape 6, 19-25
JB-9 Shape 11, 174-176
JB-10 Shape 7, 36
JB-11 Shape 7, 39
JB-12 Shape 7, 35
JB-14 Shape 7, 114
JB-15 Shape 7, 40-41
JB-16 Shape 7, 42-43
JB-17 Shape 8, 114
JB-18 Shape 7, 44-45
JB-19 Shape 7, 114
JB-20 Shape 8, 46
JB-21 Shape 8, 52-54
JB-27 Shape 10, 112-113
JB-26 Shape 10, 119-120
JB-28 Shape 9, 107-108
Jefferson 155
Jewel, The (JB-8 Shape) 22
Jewel, The (Flow Blue) ..... 33, Back Cover
Johnson, Alfred 4
Johnson, Frederick 4
Johnson, Henry 4
Johnson, Robert 4
Jolie–Pink/Multicolor 101
Juliette 161

K
Kashan 141
Katherine 161
Kensington 99
Kent 57
Kenworth (Flow Blue)
    JB-27 Shape 113
    Silver Shape ..... 51, Back Cover
Kerrydale 182
Kew Gardens 163
Khyber 15
Kildare 70

King's Road 154
Kristina 165
Kyoto 166

L
La Rochelle 27
Lace (JB-9 Shape, Oval)
    Gray & Pink 175
    Pink 175
Lace (Older, Shape Unknown)
    Gray 164
    Pink 164
Lancaster 170
Langhorn, The 21
Laurel Shape 6, 32-34
Lausanne 182
Leighton–Blue 14
Leighton–Brown 14
Leighton–Gray 14
Lemon Tree 110
Lenora 83
Liberty–Blue 103
Lichfield 70
Lincoln 155
Lindsey 141
Lombardy, The 24
London Shape 6, 26
London White 26
Lorna 141
Lorraine 138
Lothair, The
    Blue Flowers 37, 38
    Green/Gray Flowers 37
Lotus–Blue 103
Lotus–Red/Pink 103
Louisiana 187
Lucerne 159
Lucerne, The 74
Lugano 186
Lynmere 100
Lynton (Newer) 84
Lynton (Older) 150
Lyric 140

M
Madison (Heritage Shape) 109
Madison (Shape Unknown) 155
Madras, The 123
Madrid 189
Madrid, The 52
Malaga (Shape Unknown) 186
Malaga (Sovereign Shape) 82
Maldon 56
Malvern (Georgian Shape)
    Blue 80, 81
    Brown/Multicolor 80
    Plum 80
    Red 80
Malvern (Newer, Shape Unknown) 152
Malvern (Older, Old Staffordshire Shape) 69
Malvern, The 29
Manorwood 162
Margaret Rose–Brown/Multicolor 59
Margaret Rose–Green/Multicolor 59
Margaret Rose–Pink/Multicolor 59
Marie 183
Marjorie 122
Marlboro–Blue 38
Marlboro–Green 38
Marlborough 126
Marlow (Newer, Regency Shape) 99
Marlow (Old Staffordshire 1 Shape) 73
Marquis, The (JB-8 Shape) 23
Marquis, The (Old English Shape) 63
Marseilles 69

Matlock 140
Maydelle–Green 79
Mayfair (London Shape) 26
Mayfair (Shape Unknown) 125
Mayfair, The 107
Mayflower 155
McBaine 162
Meadow Brook 154
Meadow Lane 153
Meadowbrook 177
Meadowsweet 70
Meakin, James 4
Medici–Black 148
Medici–Gold 148
Medici–Red 148
Medina 162
Melba 134
Melbourne 73
Melody 98
Merry Christmas 96
Miami 138
Mikado–Green, The 33
Millstream–Blue 95
Millstream–Brown/Multicolor 95
Millstream–Pink 95
Ming 110
Minorca 122
Minuet 97
Misty 180
Misty Morning 153
Mitsouko 151
Mongolia 123
Mongolia–Blue/Gray 167
Mongolia–Flow Blue ..... 167, Back Cover
Montana–Flow Blue 48
Montana–Green 48
Monterey 183
Monterey, The 24
Monticello 28
Montpellier 27
Montrose 132
Moorland 70
Mount Vernon–Blue 80
Mount Vernon–Brown/Multicolor 80
Mount Vernon–Green/Multicolor 80
Mount Vernon–Pink 80

N
Nassau 141
Neapolitan–Blue 42
Neapolitan–Brown 42
Neapolitan–Flow Blue
    Gold Accents, No Trim ..... 42, 43, Front Cover
    No Trim 42
Neapolitan–Green 42
Neighbors 168
Netherland 133
Netherlands 139
Newark 108
Newport 33
Nicole 178
Ningpo 70
Normandy (Flow Blue) 33, 34
Norton 56
Norwood 73

O
Oakworth 132
Old Bradbury–Blue
    Cream Background 102
    White Background 102
Old Bradbury–Pink 102
Old Britain Castles (Old Staffordshire Shape)
    Pink 72

(O-S) Index

Old Britain Castles (Sovereign Shape)
Black ... 86
Blue ... 86
Brown ... 87
Brown/Multicolor ... 87
Green ... 86
Lavender ... 87
Pink ... 86, 90, Front Cover
Old Britain Castles–Pink (Christmas) ... 87
Old Chelsea Shape ... 9, 91-96
Old English Chintz (Old Staffordshire 3 Shape)
Blue/Multicolor ... 77
Lavender/Multicolor ... 77
Old English Chintz (Sovereign Shape)
Blue ... 89
Blue/Multicolor ... 89
Green/Multicolor ... 89
Lavender/Multicolor ... 89
Pink ... 89
Pink/Multicolor ... 90
Old English Clover–Brown ... 164
Old English Clover–Pink ... 164
Old English Countryside–Blue ... 88
Old English Countryside–Brown ... 88
Old English Countryside–Brown/Multicolor ... 88
Old English Countryside–Green ... 88
Old English Countryside–Pink ... 87
Old English Shape ... 8, 55-65
Old English (Scalloped) Shape ... 8, 66
Old English Trellis ... 159
Old English–White ... 66
Old Flower Prints ... 64
Old Granite Shape ... 11, 170-172
Old London–Blue ... 87
Old London–Brown/Multicolor ... 87
Old Mill–Blue, The ... 94
Old Mill–Brown, The ... 94
Old Mill–Brown/Multicolor, The ... 94
Old Mill–Pink, The ... 94
Old Mill–Purple, The ... 94
Old Staffordshire Shape ... 8, 69-72
Old Staffordshire 1 Shape ... 9, 73-74
Old Staffordshire 2 Shape ... 9, 75
Old Staffordshire 3 Shape ... 9, 76-77
Old Staffordshire–Pink ... 69
Old Staffordshire–White ... 69
Only A Rose ... 178
Ontwood ... 24
Orbit ... 157
Orchard (Old Granite Shape) ... 170
Orchard (Richmond Shape) ... 78
Orchid Splendour ... 26
Oregon (Flow Blue)
Gold Trim & Accents ... 51
No Trim ... 51
Organdy ... 149
Oriental Garden ... 172
Oriental Rose–Brown ... 79
Orkney, The ... 129
Ormsby ... 132
Otley ... 84
Oxford (Flow Blue) ... 36, Back Cover

P

Paisley–Black ... 103
Paisley–Brown ... 103
Paisley–Green ... 103
Paisley–Red ... 103
Panache ... 158
Papaya ... 186
Paper Leaves ... 152
Papyrus ... 162
Paradise (2 patterns) ... 125
Pareek Ware ... 4
Paris–Blue/Green ... 15
Paris–Brown ... 15
Park Lane ... 26
Pasadena ... 182
Pastorale Toile De Jouy–Brown ... 95
Pastorale Toile De Jouy–Brown/Multicolor ... 95
Pastorale Toile De Jouy–Green ... 94
Pastorale Toile De Jouy–Pink ... 95
Pastorale Toile De Jouy–Plum ... 95
Patchwork Farm ... 167
Patio–Blue ... 185
Patio–Brown ... 185
Peach Bloom ... 115
Peach (JB-5 Shape)
Brown ... 14
Flow Blue ... 15
Peach–Flow Blue (JB-15 Shape) ... 41
Pekin (Flow Blue) ... 53
Persian (Flow Blue) ... 53
Persian Garden ... 110
Persian Tulip–Blue ... 71, 72
Persian Tulip–Mulberry/Multicolor ... 71
Petite Fleur–Blue ... 172
Petite Fleur–Burgundy/Pink ... 172
Petroushka ... 123
Piazza ... 189
Pimlico ... 154
Pirouette ... 149
Playtime ... 190
Plaza ... 185
Plum Blossom ... 117
Plymouth ... 21
Pomona ... 65
Pontracina, The (Gold Trim) ... 148
Pontracina, The (No Trim) ... 160
Poppy ... 137
Portland ... 160
Posy ... 109
Powder Border ... 55
Prado ... 189
Prince ... 40
Prince Of Wales ... 59
Princess ... 85
Princess Mary ... 84
Provence ... 170
Provincial (Heirloom Shape) ... 27, 28
Provincial (Shape Unknown) ... 177

Q

Quadrille ... 165
Queen's Bouquet ... 62

R

Raleigh (JB-6 Shape)
Gold Trim ... 68
No Trim ... 67
Raleigh (Shape Unknown) ... 143
Rambler Rose ... 63
Ramsey ... 151
Ranelagh ... 60
Ravary ... 83
Redcliffe ... 137
Redditch ... 137
Regency ... 97
Regency Shape ... 9, 97-106
Regent, The (JB-8 Shape) ... 21
Regent, The (Laurel Shape) ... 32
Regent–Aqua ... 48
Regent–Flow Blue
Gold Trim & Verge ... 48
Gold Trim ... 48
Regis–Blue ... 33
Regis–Green ... 33
Reliance ... 123
Retford ... 159
Revere ... 109
Richmond (Flow Blue) ... 68, Back Cover
Richmond Hill ... 26
Richmond Shape ... 9, 78
Richmond White ... 78
Rio Verde ... 190
Rita ... 133
River Scenes ... 162
Riviera ... 22
Road Home, The ... 85
Road to Windsor–Red ... 88
Rolland–Blue/Green ... 50
Rolland–Green ... 50
Roman Shape ... 6, 116
Romance (Shape Unknown) ... 183
Romance (Sovereign Shape) ... 82
Romance Of The Sea ... 175
Rose Bouquet–Blue ... 101
Rose Bouquet–Pink ... 101
Rose Chintz–Blue ... 93
Rose Chintz–Pink ... 93
Rose Cloud ... 174
Rose Garden ... 102
Rosedale ... 15
Rosedawn (JB-8 Shape) ... 19
Rosedawn (Old Staffordshire Shape) ... 69
Rossmore ... 137
Rouen ... 74
Roulette ... 157
Roulette Shape ... 10, 157
Royal Homes Of Britain (Regency Shape)
Red ... 104
Royal Homes Of Britain (Sovereign Shape)
Blue ... 86
Red ... 86
Royal Warrant ... 5
Royston (Flow Blue) ... 112, Back Cover
Russell, The ... 23
Ruth–Blue/Green ... 29
Ruth–Green ... 29
Rutland ... 83

S

Sahara ... 189
Salem ... 171
Samba ... 182
San Remo ... 189
Sandlewood ... 186
Sandringham ... 110
Sanoma ... 38
Satsouma ... 125
Savannah–Green ... 46
Savannah–Purple ... 46
Savoy (Flow Blue, Elite Shape) ... 31
Savoy (JB-16 Shape)
Blue/Green ... 43
Flow Blue ... 43
Savoy–Multicolor (Newer) ... 115
Saxony ... 103
Scandia ... 117
Scarabee ... 123
Seafare ... 175, 194
Seaside ... 164
Senora–Blue ... 148
Senora–Green ... 148
Seville ... 133
Shalford ... 137
Sheldon Charcoal ... 160
Sheraton (Old Chelsea Shape) ... 93
Sheraton (Shape Unknown) ... 135
Sheringham ... 115
Shower Of Roses ... 174
Sicily ... 83
Sierra (Beige, Earthenware) ... 186
Sierra (White & Yellow Flowers) ... 182
Silhouette ... 117

Index (S-Z, Unidentified Patterns)

Silver Shape 8, 49-51
Simplicity–Blue 186
Simplicity–Red 185
Simplon, The 31
Sirocco 180
Sloane Square 152
Snow Crystals–Blue 190
Snow Crystals–Pink 175
Somerton 163
Sonata 110
Sonoma 177
Sovereign 82
Sovereign Shape 9, 82-90
Spring 105
Spring Day 153
Spring Impressions 26
Spring Medley 151
Spring Morning 110
Springfield (Richmond Shape) 78
Springfield (Shape Unknown) 162
Springtime (Sovereign Shape) 83
Springtime (Shape Unknown) 184
St. Cloud 124
St. Elmo Shape 7, 37-38
St. Louis (Flow Blue) 48
Stafford 107
Staffordshire Bouquet 100
Staffordshire Gardens 153
Stanhope 107
Stanley (Flow Blue) 68
Stratford Pink 160
Straw Hat 153
Strawberry Fair 91
Strawberry Fayre 99
Strawberry Fields 163
Strawmarket 181
Sugar & Spice–Blue 4413 171
Sugar & Spice–Brown 4413 172
Sultana 123
Sultana–Blue 139
Sultana–Blue/Green 139
Summer 71
Summer Chintz 98
Summer Chintz (All Over Design) 102
Summer Delight 159
Summer Gold 187
Summerfields 158
Summertime 180
Sun Up 170
Susanna 93
Sweet Briar 22
Sweetbriar 102
Sylvan 150
Sylvan–Blue 14
Sylvan–Brown 14
Sylvan–Brown/Multicolor 14

T

Tally Ho 96
Tarifa, The 138
Tea Leaf 163
Thistle 98
Tiffany Menagerie 167
Titania–Blue 176
Tivoli Shape 11, 185
Tivoli–White 185
Tokio (Flow Blue, JB-10 Shape) 4, 36
Tokio (Shape Unknown)
  Blue/Gray, Gold Trim 125
  Flow Blue, Gold Trim 125
  Flow Blue, No Trim 166
Touraine 32
Tower Bridge 190
Tracy 158
Trent Sanitary Works 4
Trieste, The (Flow Blue)
  Gold Trim 148, Back Cover
  No Trim 161
Tropicanna 26
Tudor Flowers 165
Tulip (Flow Blue) 41
Tulip Time–Blue (JB-8 Shape) 24
Tulip Time (Regency Shape)
  Blue 104
  Brown/Multicolor 104
Tunstall 5
Turin–Blue (Flow Blue) 142, Back Cover
Tuscany, The 37
Twelve Days Of Christmas 165, 194
Twyford 139

V

VanBuskirk, William H. 5
Variations 189
Venetian R12664 99
Venetian–Blue/Green 48
Venice–Blue/Gray 40
Venice–Flow Blue 40
Verona (Shape Unknown, Gold Trim) 140
Verona (Shape Unknown, No Trim) 189
Veronese 24
Victoria 22
Victorian Christmas 165
Vigo, The (Old English Shape) 62
Vigo, The (Shape Unknown) 124
Viking (Athena) Shape 10, 117-118
Villa 122
Villiers, The 160
Vincent 119
Vintage (Laurel Shape)
  Blue Ivy 33
  Blue/Green Ivy 33
Vintage (Old Chelsea Shape) 91
Vintage (Old English Scalloped Shape) 66
Vogue 173
Vogue (Older) 122

W

Wakefield 79
Waldorf 115
Warwick–Brown/Multicolor 79
Warwick–Mulberry 79
Warwick–Pink 79
Washington CS104-62 140
Waterfall 161
Waterford-Wedgwood Group 5
Watermill–Brown 106
Watteau
  Tan Scrolls & Dots Border 137
  Yellow Ovals Border 137
Waverley 67
Wedgwood Group 5
Wentworth 24
Westbourne 143
Wheat 188
Whitehall 146
Wild Cherries 158
Wild Flowers 151
Wild Rose 50
Wild Turkeys–Brown (Native American) 13
Wild Turkeys–Flying 13
Wildflowers 154
Wildmoor 181
Willow–Blue 168, 169
Willow–Pink/Red 168
Winchester 167
Winchester–Pink 62
Windfall 161
Windsor 115
Windsor Castle 190
Windsor Flowers 79
Windsor Fruit (Georgian Shape) 80
Windsor Fruit (Old Chelsea Shape) 94
Winter Holiday 13
Woodland 115
Woodland Wild Turkeys–Brown/Multicolor 13
Woodland Wild Turkeys–Green 13
Worcester 52

Y

Yale 22

Z

Zephyr 170

Unidentified Patterns

JB1 60
JB4 60
JB7 133
JB9 79
JB10 16
JB12 185
JB13 126
JB14 107
JB16 135
JB17 129
JB18 60
JB19 60
JB20 146
JB21 60
JB23 52
JB24 128
JB25 138
JB29 132
JB30 135
JB31 91
JB32 112
JB33 61
JB34 17
JB35 19
JB36 143
JB37 144
JB38 30
JB39 123
JB41 126
JB42 126
JB43 18
JB44 128
JB45 129
JB46 122
JB47 56
JB49 20
JB50 130
JB52 19
JB53 180
JB54 35
JB56 128
JB57 129
JB58 17
JB59 123
JB60 82
JB63 152
JB64 155
JB65 91
JB66 62
JB67 76
JB68 114
JB69 49
JB71 131
JB72 73
JB73 76, 77
JB78 133
JB79 187
JB80 174
JB81 153

(Unidentified Patterns) Index

Pattern	Page	Pattern	Page	Pattern	Page
JB82	122	JB177	119	JB285	75
JB83	56	JB178	44	JB286	145
JB84	20	JB179	30	JB287	125
JB86	85	JB181	18	JB288	131
JB89	143	JB182	156	JB291	44
JB90	124	JB183	135	JB292	179
JB91	150	JB184	16	JB293	17
JB92	133	JB185	128	JB295	114
JB93	49	JB189	139	JB298	140
JB94	57	JB189–Cream	139	JB301	144
JB95	144	JB190	49	JB303	131
JB99	144	JB191	145	JB304	114
JB100	58	JB193	140	JB305	55
JB101	20	JB195	136	JB306	114
JB102	133	JB196	128	JB307	52
JB103	112	JB197	112	JB308	157
JB104	136	JB198	154	JB309	98
JB105	112	JB201	127	JB311	126
JB106	35	JB203	114	JB313	47
JB107	156	JB204	153	JB314	35
JB108	47	JB205	129	JB316	145
JB109	144	JB206	107	JB318	121
JB111	40	JB207–Blue	69	JB320	20
JB112	143	JB207–Green	69	JB321	156
JB114	126	JB209	29	JB322	121
JB116	156	JB210	60	JB323	117
JB117	60	JB211	17	JB324	117
JB118	132	JB212	65	JB325	127
JB119	134	JB213	129	JB326	148
JB121	134	JB214	92	JB327	92
JB122	131	JB215	113	JB328	150
JB123	32	JB216	39	JB329	138
JB124	49	JB218	20	JB330	20
JB125	159	JB219	137	JB332	128
JB126	135	JB220	128	JB334	61
JB128	91	JB225	146	JB335	60
JB130	132	JB226	178	JB336	161
JB131	37	JB227	57	JB337	52
JB132	113	JB228	16	JB338	124
JB133	35	JB229	32	JB339	73
JB134	131	JB230	47	JB340	179
JB135	113	JB231	35	JB342	83
JB136	63	JB232	52	JB343	147
JB137	56	JB233	130	JB345	130
JB138	59	JB235	143	JB346	182
JB139	100	JB238	174	JB347	47
JB140	55	JB239	145	JB348	134
JB141	178	JB240	181	JB349	152
JB142	152	JB241	181	JB350	145
JB143	174	JB243	121	JB351	110
JB144	145	JB244	188	JB352	55
JB145	126	JB246	40	JB353	67
JB146	166	JB249	61	JB355	40
JB147	67, 68	JB250	47	JB356	182
JB148	156	JB251	30	JB357	149
JB150	146	JB252	67	JB358	32
JB151	146	JB253	37	JB359	19
JB155	147	JB254	21	JB361	16
JB156	147	JB255	57	JB362	121
JB157	186	JB256	63	JB364	30
JB158	188	JB257	30	JB365	18
JB159	32	JB260	84	JB366	139
JB161	73	JB261	107	JB369	49
JB162	124	JB263	119	JB370	101
JB163	29	JB264	133	JB371	175
JB164	151	JB265	128	JB372	149
JB167	135	JB267	16	JB374	136
JB168	19	JB269	35	JB377	16
JB169	61	JB270	35	JB378	112
JB170	131	JB271	91	JB380	117
JB171	130	JB273	18	JB381	92
JB172	134	JB276	112	JB382	140
JB173	147	JB278	151	JB383	16
JB174	129	JB281	130	JB385	122
JB175	112	JB284	16	JB386	181

201

Index (Unidentified Patterns)

Pattern	Page	Pattern	Page	Pattern	Page
JB387	55	JB487	185	JB597	140
JB388	44	JB488	17	JB598	40
JB391	39	JB489	85	JB601	36
JB392	91	JB490	179	JB602	99
JB395	187	JB492	119	JB603	106
JB397	31	JB493	131	JB604	42
JB398	32	JB494	113	JB605	99
JB399	76	JB495	124	JB606	71
JB400	29	JB496	39	JB607	188
JB402	177	JB497	115	JB608	181
JB403	39	JB498	97	JB611	180
JB404	56	JB499	50	JB614	156
JB406	180	JB502	178	JB617	178
JB408	36	JB503	55	JB618	29
JB409	30	JB504–Scalloped	97	JB619	150
JB410	144	JB504–Smooth	136	JB620	55
JB411	119	JB505	84	JB621	85
JB412	114	JB508	180	JB626	52
JB413	108	JB509	157	JB627	32
JB414	108	JB510	16	JB628	100
JB415	145	JB511	42	JB629	147
JB416	129	JB513	97	JB631	144
JB418	76	JB515	84	JB633	17
JB419	178	JB516	61	JB636	58
JB420	57	JB517	175	JB637	182
JB421	44	JB518	30	JB640	169
JB422	145	JB519	56	JB641	92
JB423	185	JB521	138	JB642	85
JB424	122	JB522	130	JB645	145
JB425	62	JB523	49	JB647	142
JB426	147	JB524	42	JB650	37
JB427	121	JB527	119	JB652	47
JB428	36	JB528	142	JB654	124
JB430	61	JB531	58	JB657	130
JB431	100	JB533	188	JB658	114
JB432	100	JB534	62	JB659	120
JB433	50	JB535	133	JB662	61
JB434	142	JB536	73	JB664	91
JB435	84	JB537	139	JB667	150
JB437	17	JB539	135	JB669	47
JB438	17	JB540	159	JB670	49
JB439	61	JB541	154	JB671	99
JB441	113	JB542	185	JB672	15
JB442	19	JB543	136	JB673	97
JB443	179	JB544	44	JB680	114
JB444	42	JB545	132	JB681	37
JB445	179	JB546	143	JB684	52
JB447	82	JB550	18	JB685	155
JB448	15	JB552	135	JB686	58
JB449	114	JB553	57	JB691	18
JB450	17	JB556	63	JB692	18
JB451	92	JB558	33	JB695	100
JB452	136	JB559	159	JB696	62
JB453	63	JB560	179	JB697	69
JB454	122	JB563	157	JB708	127
JB455	121	JB565	134	JB709	136
JB457	132	JB567	177	JB711	126
JB458	141	JB568	63	JB712	23
JB459	163	JB570	143	JB713	76
JB460	35	JB571	39	JB716	146
JB461	121	JB572	85	JB718	76
JB462	150	JB574	130	JB720	108
JB463	44	JB575	67	JB724	126
JB470	141	JB576	20	JB728	75
JB472	166	JB578	67	JB729	113
JB473	146	JB579	138	JB730	136
JB474	32	JB582	136	JB732	146
JB475	76	JB583	63	JB733	58
JB477	125	JB585	107	JB735	130
JB479	179	JB586	49	JB743	176
JB481	29	JB588	29	JB746	174
JB482	99	JB589	55	JB749	134
JB483	91	JB592	52	JB752	129
JB485	15	JB593	76	JB753	121
JB486	62	JB595	151		

About the Authors

Bob, Owen, Dale and Ryan
Photography: Donna Pickerel, School Pictures, Inc.

Bob Page was born April 19, 1945 and grew up working the fields of his family's small tobacco farm in Ruffin, North Carolina. He attended the University of North Carolina at Chapel Hill and graduated with a degree in business and a major in accounting. After two years in the U.S. Army, he obtained his CPA certificate and worked in public accounting for eight years. In 1978, he took a position as an auditor for the State of North Carolina.

In March of 1981, Bob left his accounting career forever to form Replacements, Ltd. He and his company have received extensive publicity and public recognition. Awards include: The North Carolina Excellence Award presented by Governor James Martin; North Carolina Small Businessman of the Year; a ranking of #81 in Inc. magazine's annual list of America's fastest growing privately held companies (1986); North Carolina Person of the Week from UNC Center for Public Television; and 1991 Retail Entrepreneur of the Year for the State of North Carolina. In 1998, Bob received the National Partnership for Progress Award from the U.S. Postmaster General. Bob is involved in numerous charitable endeavors in North Carolina as well as the nation and is also a tireless advocate for the rights of gay and lesbian individuals. Bob was named one of America's Top 25 "Out" Executives in 1999. He also won the Human Rights Campaign's Torch Award in 1996.

Dale Frederiksen was born June 15, 1962 in Pontiac, Michigan and attended Waterford Township High School. In 1980, Dale moved to Chattanooga, Tennessee to attend Tennessee Temple University, graduating in 1984 with a BS degree in secondary education. He taught junior and senior high mathematics for three years in Kansas City, Kansas, returning to Chattanooga in 1987 to teach mathematics and to coach volleyball at Ooltewah Middle School.

In 1989, he joined the staff of Replacements, Ltd. as an inventory purchasing agent and is currently involved in the creation and production of various china, crystal and silver identification guides. Dale enjoys researching and discovering patterns that have previously been undocumented, along with spending time with his partner Bob and their twin boys — Owen and Ryan.

The History of
REPLACEMENTS, LTD.

The World's Largest Retailer of Old and New China, Crystal, Silver and Collectibles

The Replacements, Ltd. Museum

One of Replacements' collectibles showcases

Inside the 225,000 sq. ft. warehouse

Our careful inspection of china

An overhead view of Replacements, Ltd.

Our careful inspection of crystal

In 1981, Bob Page, an accountant-turned-flea-marketer, founded Replacements, Ltd. Since then, the company's growth and success can only be described as phenomenal.

Today, Replacements, Ltd. locates hard-to-find pieces in over 180,000 patterns — some of which have not been produced for more than 100 years. Now serving more than 5 million customers, with an inventory of 9.5 million pieces, they mail and e-mail up to 800,000 inventory listings weekly to customers seeking additional pieces in their patterns.

The concept for Replacements, Ltd. originated in the late 1970's when Page, then an auditor for the state of North Carolina, started spending his weekends combing flea markets buying china and crystal. Before long, he was filling requests from customers to find pieces they could not locate. "I was buying and selling pieces primarily as a diversion," Page explains. "Back when I was an auditor, no one was ever happy to see me. And, quite frankly, I wasn't thrilled about being there either."

Page began placing small ads in shelter publications and started building a file of potential customers. Soon, his inventory outgrew his attic, where he had been storing the pieces, and it was time to make a change. "I reached the point where I was spending more time with dishes than auditing," Page says. "I'd be up until one or two o'clock in the morning. Finally, I took the big step — I quit my auditing job and hired one part-time assistant. Today I'm having so much fun, I often have to remind myself what day of the week it is!"

Replacements, Ltd. continued to grow quickly. In fact, in 1986, Inc. magazine ranked Replacements, Ltd. 81st on its list of fastest-growing independently-owned companies in the U.S. "Our growth has been incredible," says Page, who was named 1991 North

A view of Replacements' 12,000 square foot Showroom.

Carolina Entrepreneur of the Year. "I had no idea of the potential when I started out."

Providing high-quality merchandise and the highest possible levels of customer service are the corner-stones of the business, resulting in a shopping experience unparalleled in today's marketplace. Page also attributes much of the success of Replacements, Ltd. to a network of about 1,000 dedicated suppliers from all around the U.S. The company currently employs more than 550 people in an expanded 225,000 square foot facility (the size of four football fields).

Another major contributor to the company's fast growth and top-level customer service is the extensive computer system used to keep track of the inventory. This state-of-the-art system also stores customer files, including requests for specific pieces in their patterns. It is maintained by a full-time staff of 20 people and is constantly upgraded to ensure customers receive the information they desire quickly and accurately.

For those who are unsure of the name and/or manufacturer of their patterns, Replacements, Ltd. also offers a free pattern identification service. In addition, numerous books and publications focusing on pattern identification have been published by Replacements, Ltd. for both suppliers and individuals.

Replacements, Ltd. receives countless phone calls and letters from its many satisfied customers. Some need to replace broken or lost items while others want to supplement the sets they have had for years. A constant in the varied subjects customers write about is their long and fruitless search — a search that ended when they learned what Replacements, Ltd. could offer. "Since many patterns are family heirlooms that have been handed down from generation to generation, most customers are sentimental about replacing broken or missing pieces," Page says. "It's a great feeling to help our customers replace pieces in their patterns and to be able to see their satisfaction. Like our logo says — We Replace the Irreplaceable."

Another growing area that Replacements, Ltd. has developed for its customers is the collectibles market. The company now offers a wide range of collectibles from companies such as Bing and Grondahl, Royal Copenhagen, Boehm, Hummel, Lladro and many more. "It was a natural progression of our business," says Page, "and something our customers had been requesting."

The Replacements, Ltd. Showroom and Museum in Greensboro, NC is a 12,000 square-foot retail facility located in front of the massive warehouse. It is decorated with late 19th century hand-carved showcases, 20-foot ceilings and classic chandeliers. Inside, one can view an incredibly varied selection of merchandise — from figurines, mugs and ornaments to the china, crystal and silver that made the company famous.

The fascinating Replacements, Ltd. Museum, adjacent to the retail Showroom, is the home for over 2,000 rare and unusual pieces that Page has collected over the years. It includes a special section dedicated to one of Page's first loves — early 20th century glass from companies such as Tiffin, Fostoria, Heisey, Imperial and Cambridge.

Some of the 50,000 shelves which hold over 9.5 million pieces of inventory.

For More Information

- Call 1-800-REPLACE (1-800-737-5223) from 8 am to midnight, Eastern Time, 7 days a week).
- Write to: 1089 Knox Road
  PO Box 26029
  Greensboro, NC 27420
- Fax: 336-697-3100
- Internet: www.replacements.com
- Visit the Replacements, Ltd. Showroom and Museum, at exit 132 off I-85/40 in Greensboro, NC. The Showroom and Museum are open 7 days a week, from 9 am to 8 pm.

Publication Pricing

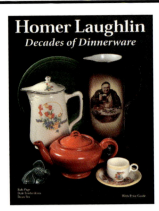

**Homer Laughlin
Decades of Dinnerware**
The definitive book on Homer Laughlin dinnerware featuring more than 3,000 patterns in full color. Pre-1900 to current Fiesta® patterns and everything in between. Plus a separate price guide! Hardcover, 559 pages.
Retail $39.95   Our Price **$29.99**

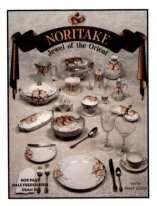

**Noritake
Jewel of the Orient**
Includes Noritake patterns produced prior to 1960. Full-color digital images organized for identification. Company history and price guide included. Hardcover, 321 pages.
Retail $29.95   Our Price **$27.99**

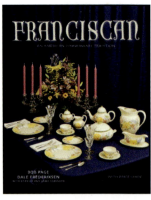

**Franciscan–An American
Dinnerware Tradition**
The foremost comprehensive book on Franciscan dinnerware. Full-color, beautifully designed for identification. Includes company history and price guide. Hardcover, 272 pages.
Retail $29.95   Our Price **$27.99**

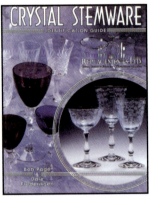

Crystal Stemware Identification Guide
The most extensive guide to crystal stemware ever published. Covers over 200 manufacturers with more than 4,000 illustrations of today's most popular crystal patterns. Softbound, 372 pages.
Retail $18.95   Our Price **$12.99**

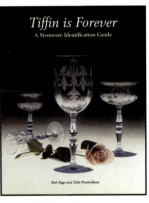

**Tiffin Is Forever
A Guide to Tiffin Crystal**
This helpful guide includes comprehensive, detailed illustrations of over 2,700 stems and patterns of Tiffin Glass. A must for the glass enthusiast or collector. Hardcover, 175 pages.
Retail $29.95   Our Price **$19.99**

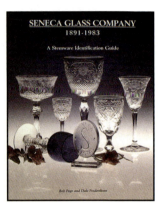

Seneca Glass Company: 1891-1983
Includes information on over 1,200 different stems and patterns, along with a history of the Seneca Glass Company by West Virginia glass authority Dean Six. Hardcover, 132 pages.
Retail $24.95   Our Price **$17.99**

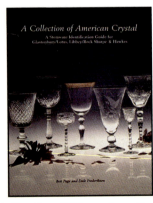

A Collection Of American Crystal
Includes descriptions of crystal by Glastonbury/Lotus, Libbey/Rock Sharpe, and the TG Hawkes glass companies. Over 1,000 patterns and 200 stems. Hardcover, 140 pages.
Retail $24.95   Our Price **$17.99**

Stainless Flatware Guide
More than 5,000 stainless patterns from over 100 manufacturers. Over 700 pages of highly detailed, digitally captured images organized by shape and style. Softbound, 798 pages.
Retail $39.95   Our Price **$24.99**

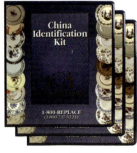

China ID Kits
Various companies featured in each kit. Quickly identify patterns with full-color and black & white images and easy to use tabs. Looseleaf, page count varies. KIT #1: Denby, Easterling, Flintridge, Gorham, Johann Haviland, Longchamp, Royal Jackson, Royal Tettau, and Syracuse. KIT #2: Adams, Arabia, Crown Ducal, Franconia, Gold Castle, Midwinter, Pfaltzgraff, and Winfield. KIT #3: Corning, Dansk, Independence, Iroquois, Lefton, and Nikko.
Retail $59.95   Our Price **$49.99**

Publication Pricing

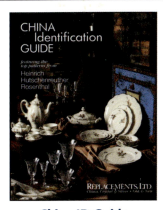

China ID Guide
(Heinrich, Hutschenreuther, Rosenthal)

Featuring over 900 of the top patterns of these manufacturers. Digitally captured images are organized by shape and style. Softbound, 120 pages.

Retail **$59.95**   Our Price **$29.99**

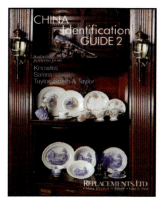

China ID Guide 2
(Knowles, Salem, Taylor, Smith & Taylor)

Featuring over 1,100 digitally captured images of the most popular patterns produced by Edwin M. Knowles, Salem, and Taylor, Smith & Taylor. Softbound, 144 pages.

Retail **$59.95**   Our Price **$29.99**

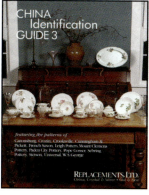

China ID Guide 3
(Canonsburg, Cronin, Crooksville, Cunningham & Pickett, French Saxon, Leigh Potters, Mount Clemens Pottery, Paden City Pottery, Pope Gosser, Sebring Pottery, Stetson, Universal, W.S. George)

Over 1,400 digitally captured images arranged by shape and style. Softbound, 213 pages.

Retail **$59.95**   Our Price **$29.99**

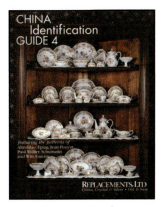

China ID Guide 4
(Altrohlau, Epiag, Jean Pouyat, Paul Müller, Schumann, and Wm. Guerin)

Over 1,200 digitally captured images of these European manufacturers arranged by shape and style. Softbound, 165 pages.

Retail **$59.95**   Our Price **$29.99**

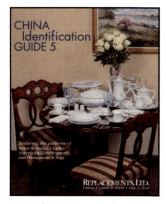

China ID Guide 5
(Bawo & Dotter, Charles Ahrenfeldt, Tirschenreuth, and Tressemann & Vogt)

Over 1,400 digitally captured images of these European manufacturers arranged by shape and style. Softbound, 187 pages.

Retail **$59.95**   Our Price **$29.99**

China ID Guide 6
(Arcadian, Harker, Limoges (American), Princess, Royal, Shenango, Steubenville, and Warwick)

Over 1,400 digitally captured images of these American manufacturers arranged by shape and style. Softbound, 197 pages.

Retail **$59.95**   Our Price **$29.99**

China ID Guide 7
(MEITO, Celebrate, Craftsman, Diamond, Empress, Hira, Imperial, Jyoto, National, Princess, Regal)

Patterns for these Japanese manufacturers are featured (concentrating on Meito) with over 1,700 digitally captured images. Softbound, 219 pages.

Retail **$39.99**   Our Price **$29.99**

REPLACEMENTS, LTD.
China, Crystal & Silver • Old & New

To order:
**Call 1-800-REPLACE
(1-800-737-5223)**
Outside the USA: (1-336-697-3000)

Or visit us on the web at:
www.replacements.com®

Additional Resource

Mary Finegan is a Johnson Brothers dinnerware pioneer and expert. Her efforts to chronicle and document the production and history of Johnson Brothers china led the way with the first book on the topic in 1993. She has been to England several times to tour and gather information, producing a second book in 2003 with 158 pages of history text, period ads, and much more. We confidently recommend Mary's book for more in-depth information on Johnson Brothers.

**To order Mary Finegan's book, please contact her at:
www.johnsonbrothersbook.com.**

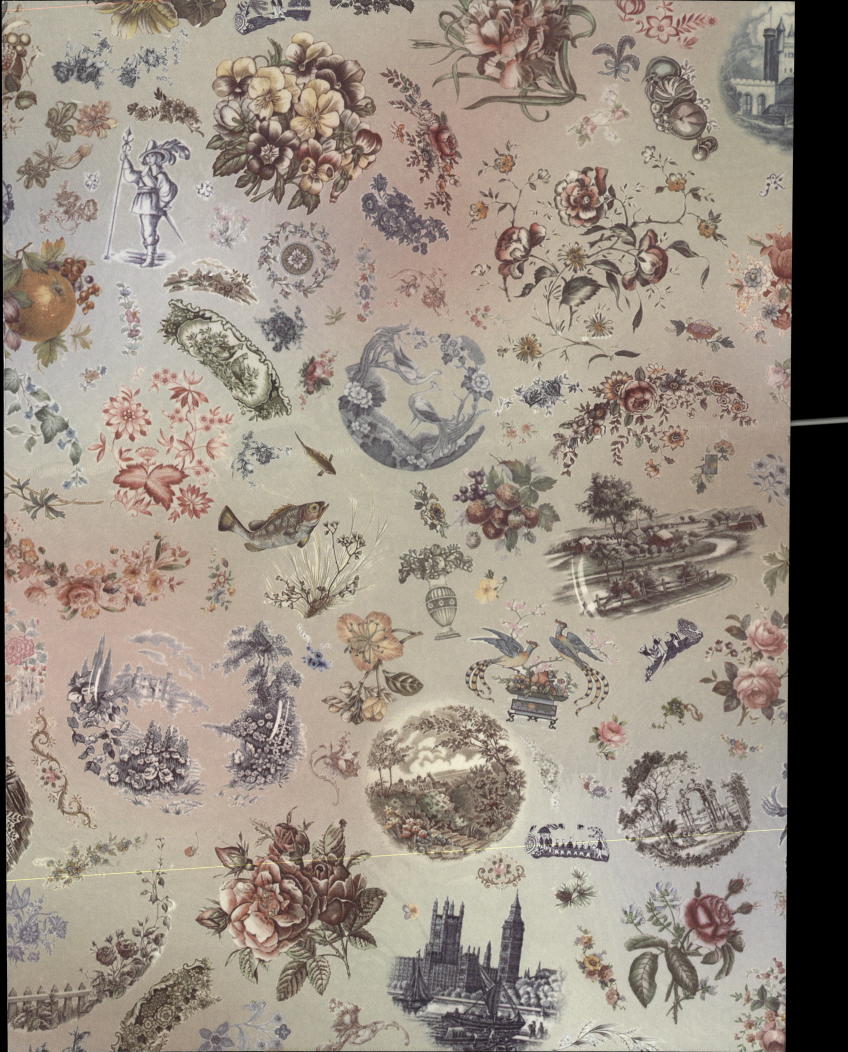